Python 10

Introduction

What is Python?

Python is a versatile and powerful programming language that has gained immense popularity since its inception in the late 1980s. Designed by Guido van Rossum and first released in 1991, Python emphasizes code readability and simplicity, making it an excellent choice for both beginner and experienced programmers. At its core, Python's design philosophy revolves around the principle of readability, using indentation and whitespace to structure code, which in turn makes it easier to write and understand.

One of the key features of Python is its dynamic typing and interpreted nature. Unlike statically typed languages, where each variable must be declared and assigned a type before use, Python variables can hold data of any type and can change type dynamically. This allows for greater flexibility and ease of use, especially during development and prototyping phases.

Python's extensive standard library is another significant advantage. With a rich set of modules and packages, Python provides tools for various applications, ranging from data manipulation, web development, and machine learning, to scientific computing and automation. The phrase "batteries included" aptly describes Python's standard library, as it comes with modules for handling common programming tasks, negating the need to write code from scratch for routine operations.

Moreover, Python has a vibrant and supportive community. From online forums and user groups to comprehensive documentation and tutorials, resources for learning and troubleshooting are readily available. This community-driven approach ensures that Python remains updated, with regular releases that introduce new features and improve performance.

Python's flexibility extends to its use in different programming paradigms. Whether you're interested in object-oriented programming, functional programming, or procedural programming, Python supports all these paradigms and allows you to choose the most suitable one for your project.

In practical terms, Python is often lauded for its role in data science and artificial intelligence. Libraries such as NumPy, pandas, and scikit-learn have cemented Python's place as the go-to language for data analysis. Simultaneously, frameworks like TensorFlow and PyTorch make it easier for developers to create complex machine learning models.

Web developers also find Python beneficial, thanks to powerful frameworks like Django and Flask that simplify the process of building robust and scalable web applications. These frameworks provide essential tools and patterns for web development, allowing developers to focus more on the application's functionality rather than boilerplate code.

In summary, Python's simplicity, readability, extensive libraries, and supportive community make it an appealing choice for a wide range of programming tasks. Whether you're just starting your coding journey or you're a seasoned developer, Python offers a harmonious blend of ease-of-use and powerful features, making it a valuable addition to your programming toolkit.

History and Evolution

Python, a versatile and powerful programming language, has a fascinating history marked by continuous evolution and community-driven development. Its journey began in late 1989 when Guido van Rossum, a Dutch programmer, decided to work on a hobby project to keep himself occupied during the Christmas holidays. Guido aimed to create a language that would bridge the gap between the high-level and low-level programming worlds, prioritizing readability and simplicity.

Van Rossum drew inspiration from the ABC language, a teaching language he had previously worked on at the Centrum Wiskunde & Informatica (CWI) in the Netherlands. While ABC was designed for teaching programming concepts, it lacked the flexibility and appeal needed for more extensive use. Guido envisioned a language that embraced the best features of ABC while remedying its shortcomings. His project was named "Python," a playful nod to the British comedy series "Monty Python's Flying Circus," which Guido was a fan of.

The early 1990s saw the first public release of Python. Version 0.9.0 was released in February 1991 and included many of the features that we recognize today, such as exception handling, functions, and the core data types like lists and strings. From its inception, Python's design philosophy emphasized code readability and simplicity, embodied in the guiding principles outlined in "The Zen of Python," authored by Tim Peters.

Python's first official version, Python 1.0, was released in January 1994. This version introduced new features like lambda, map, filter, and reduce, which reflected the language's growing capabilities. Despite its initial modest adoption, Python gradually gained traction among programmers who appreciated its clean syntax and versatility.

The late 1990s and early 2000s were pivotal for Python's development. In 2000, Python 2.0 was released, a significant milestone that introduced list comprehensions and a garbage collection system capable of automatic memory management. This period also saw the formation of the Python Software Foundation (PSF), a non-profit organization established to manage the open-source licensing and oversee Python's development.

Python 2.0 marked the start of a golden era for Python, but it wasn't without its challenges. The language's growth spurt came with the accumulation of legacy features and inconsistencies, prompting the need for a more elegant solution. This led to the ambitious development of Python 3.0, released in December 2008. Python 3.0, also known as "Python 3000" or "Py3k," was not backward compatible with Python 2.x. This major release aimed to rectify fundamental design flaws and streamline the language.

Python 3 introduced several improvements: a more consistent and clear syntax, enhanced standard library, and the unification of types and classes into a single hierarchy. The print statement was replaced with the print() function, integer division was standardized, and Unicode became the default string format, reflecting a more modern and global approach to programming.

The transition from Python 2.x to Python 3.x was gradual, with many projects hesitating to migrate due to the incompatibility issues. Consequently, support for Python 2.x continued for several years, with the final release, Python 2.7, maintained until January 1, 2020. Since then, Python 3.x has become the standard, and the community has shifted focus to improving features and expanding its capabilities.

Today, Python is renowned for its applicability in various fields, from web development and data science to artificial intelligence and scientific computing. The language's success is a testament to its robust, adaptive nature and the vibrant community that continues to refine and expand it. Python's journey from a holiday project to a global programming phenomenon underscores the power of thoughtful design and community collaboration in shaping technological evolution.

Why Learn Python?

When it comes to programming languages, Python is often touted as one of the best beginners' languages out there—and for good reason. Whether you're a complete novice or a seasoned programmer looking to expand your skill set, Python offers a versatile and intuitive platform for bringing your ideas to life.

First and foremost, let's talk about simplicity and readability. Python's syntax is designed to be easy to read and write, which means you can spend less time worrying about tricky syntax errors and more time focusing on solving problems. This attribute makes Python exceptionally accessible, even for people who may not consider themselves to be "tech-savvy."

Another compelling reason to learn Python is its massive and supportive community. The Python ecosystem is rich with resources, from extensive documentation to forums, tutorials, and local Python meetups. No matter what challenge you're facing, chances are someone has encountered it before and has shared a solution online.

Python is also incredibly versatile. It's not just limited to web or software development. Python is widely used in data analysis, artificial intelligence, machine learning, automation, web scraping, game development, and more. Its extensive libraries and frameworks, such as Pandas for data manipulation, TensorFlow for machine learning, and Django for web development, mean that Python can be your one-stop-shop for a wide array of programming needs.

Moreover, Python is highly popular in academia and industry alike. Many educational institutions use Python as a teaching tool because it allows students to pick up the fundamentals quickly. Similarly, large tech companies like Google, Facebook, and Netflix use Python extensively in their operations. Learning Python can therefore open doors to various career paths in tech.

Another aspect worth mentioning is Python's ability to interface with other programming languages and systems. Whether you need to integrate with C/C++, use tools from the Java ecosystem, or run scripts on a .NET framework, Python has the capability to play well with others. This makes it an excellent tool for both beginners and experienced developers who need to integrate different technologies.

Lastly, Python is an excellent tool for prototyping. Its ease of use and rapid development cycle allow developers to create prototypes quickly and iterate as needed. This speeds up the development process and allows for more innovation and creativity.

In summary, learning Python offers a plethora of benefits, from an easy-to-understand syntax and strong community support to its versatility and flexibility in various fields and applications. Whether you're looking to pursue a career in tech, automate everyday tasks, or simply experiment with coding, Python provides a dynamic and robust platform to achieve your goals.

Setting Up the Python Environment

Before diving into the world of Python programming, it's essential to prepare your development environment properly. Having the right setup will make your learning experience smoother and more enjoyable. In this section, we'll walk you through installing Python, setting up a text editor, and configuring your first project.

Installing Python

Python is a versatile language used in various fields, from web development to data science. To start coding in Python, the first step is to install the Python interpreter on your machine. Head over to the official Python website and download the latest version of Python that suits your operating system—whether you're using Windows, macOS, or Linux. During installation, make sure to check the box that says "Add Python to PATH"; this will allow you to run Python from any command prompt or terminal window.

Choosing the Right Text Editor or IDE

Choosing a text editor or Integrated Development Environment (IDE) largely depends on your preferences and requirements. Here's a brief overview of some popular options:

- **VS Code**: Visual Studio Code is a free, open-source text editor developed by Microsoft. It offers a rich ecosystem of extensions and integrates well with Python. Its features include syntax highlighting, debugging, and version control.

- **PyCharm**: JetBrains' PyCharm is a robust IDE specifically designed for Python. It offers a plethora of features, including code navigation, refactoring tools, and integrated testing capabilities. While PyCharm has a free Community Edition, the Professional Edition offers even more advanced features.

- **Sublime Text**: Sublime Text is another popular text editor known for its speed and simplicity. It has numerous plugins for Python development and a very user-friendly interface.

- **Jupyter Notebook**: For those interested in data science, Jupyter Notebooks offer a unique interface to write and execute Python code in the same document. This tool is especially useful for data analysis and visualization.

Writing Your First Python Program

Once you have installed Python and chosen your preferred editor, it's time to write your first Python program! Open your text editor or IDE, create a new file, and save it with a .py extension (for example, `hello_world.py`). In the file, type the following code:

```python
print("Hello, World!")
```

To run your program, open your terminal or command prompt, navigate to the directory where your file is saved, and type:

```sh
python hello_world.py
```

If everything is set up correctly, you should see "Hello, World!" displayed in your terminal.

Virtual Environments (Optional but Recommended)

As you delve deeper into Python, you'll encounter projects with different dependencies. Managing these dependencies can be tricky, so it's highly recommended to use virtual environments. A virtual environment is an isolated space where you can install packages without affecting the global Python installation.

To create a virtual environment, navigate to your project directory and run:

```sh
python -m venv myenv
```

Activate the virtual environment with:

- On Windows:
  ```sh
  myenv\Scripts\activate
  ```

- On macOS and Linux:
  ```sh
  source myenv/bin/activate
  ```

You can now install project-specific packages using pip without worrying about conflicts with other projects.

Conclusion

Setting up your Python environment might seem like a chore, but it's a crucial first step on your programming journey. With Python installed, a good text editor in place, and your first program executed successfully, you are well on your way to becoming proficient in Python. The next steps will delve into the language's syntax, data structures, and many more exciting topics. Happy coding!

Your First Python Program

Imagine you've just opened the door to a new world, a world where you can bring your ideas to life through code. Python, a welcoming language with its simple and readable syntax, is like a friendly guide on this journey. Let's start by writing your very first Python program.

To begin, you'll need to have Python installed on your computer. You can download it from the official Python website and follow the installation instructions there. Once you have Python set up, you'll also need a place to write your code. This could be a simple text editor like Notepad on Windows, TextEdit on Mac, or more advanced integrated development environments (IDEs) like PyCharm or Visual Studio Code.

Now, let's dive into the code. Open your text editor or IDE and create a new file. Name it `hello.py`. The `.py` extension tells your computer that this file contains Python code.

In your new `hello.py` file, type the following line:

```python
print("Hello, World!")
```

This line of code is your first step into the world of Python programming. But what does it do? Let's break it down:

1. `print`: This is a built-in function in Python. Functions are like commands that tell the computer to do something specific. The `print` function tells the computer to display some text on the screen.
2. `"Hello, World!"`: This is a string, a sequence of characters enclosed in quotation marks. In this case, it's a friendly greeting to the world.

When you run your program, the `print` function will output the string "Hello, World!" to the screen.

To run your program, save your file and open a terminal or command prompt. Navigate to the directory (folder) where you saved `hello.py` and type:

```sh
python hello.py
```

Then press Enter. You should see the text `Hello, World!` appear. Congratulations, you've just written and executed your first Python program!

This simple program might seem trivial at first glance, but it carries a lot of significance. It's like the first brick laid in the foundation of a grand building. With this foundational knowledge, you're equipped to start exploring more complex structures in Python. From here, you can build more complicated programs that can solve problems, analyze data, and even create games.

Let's take a moment to reflect on what you've accomplished. By running this tiny snippet of code, you've engaged with several important concepts of programming: creating a file, writing a function, and executing a file. These are fundamental skills you will build upon as you continue your Python journey.

Remember, every expert in Python began with this small step. Each line of code you write from now on will add to your understanding and capability. Exciting new challenges and discoveries lie ahead, and it all began with those two powerful words: `print("Hello, World!")`. Welcome to the world of Python programming!

Chapter 1: Basics of Python

Variables and Data Types

In the fascinating world of Python, the concept of variables and data types forms the bedrock of programming. This foundational knowledge will enable you to create dynamic and functional scripts.

Variables

Think of variables as containers that store data values. When you create a variable in Python, you give it a name and assign it a value. Naming a variable is essential because it makes your code more readable and maintainable.

Let's look at an example:

```python
age = 25
name = "Alice"
is_student = True
```

In this snippet, `age` is a variable storing the integer value 25, `name` holds the string "Alice", and `is_student` is a Boolean set to True. Notice the equal sign (`=`) used for assignment. Unlike some other programming languages, Python does not require you to declare the type of variable explicitly. The type is automatically inferred from the value you assign to it.

Data Types

Python supports several data types, each serving a specific purpose. Understanding these types is crucial for writing efficient and error-free code.

Integers

Integers are whole numbers, positive or negative.

```python
num1 = 10
num2 = -5
```

Floating-Point Numbers

Floating-point numbers are real numbers with a decimal point.

```python
temperature = 98.6
height = 5.9
```

Strings

Strings are sequences of characters enclosed in quotes, either single or double.

```python
greeting = "Hello, World!"
char = 'A'
```

Booleans

Booleans represent one of two values: True or False.

```python
is_raining = False
passed_exam = True
```

Type Conversion

Sometimes, you may need to convert a variable from one type to another. Python provides several built-in functions for type conversion.

- `int()` converts to an integer
- `float()` converts to a floating-point number

- `str()` converts to a string

Here's how you can perform type conversion:

```python
# Converting a float to an integer
num = int(9.8)  # num will be 9

# Converting an integer to a string
text = str(123)  # text will be '123'

# Converting a string to a float
price = float("49.99")  # price will be 49.99
```

Variable Naming Rules

While Python is relatively lenient in terms of variable naming, adhering to some rules and conventions is good practice:

1. Names must begin with a letter (a-z, A-Z) or an underscore (_).
2. Names can only contain letters, numbers, and underscores (no spaces or special characters like %, &, etc.).
3. Names are case-sensitive (`name`, `Name`, and `NAME` are different variables).

Here are some valid and invalid variable names:

```python
# Valid names
first_name = "John"
_daysInWeek = 7
temperature2 = 23


# Invalid names
2nd_place = "silver"  # Variable name cannot start with a number
first-name = "Alice"  # Hyphens are not allowed
total$amount = 100  # Special characters are not allowed
```

Best Practices for Naming
1. Use descriptive names to convey the purpose of the variable.
2. Follow the convention of using lowercase words separated by underscores (snake_case).

Avoid using single-letter variable names except for in contexts like loop counters, where their purpose is perfectly clear. Descriptive names make your code more readable and easier to debug.

```python
# Poor naming
x = 10
y = 20

# Better naming
num_apples = 10
num_oranges = 20
```

Understanding and effectively using variables and data types is the first step toward mastering Python. As you continue your Python journey, these basic concepts will become the building blocks for more complex and powerful applications.

Basic Operators

In our journey to master Python, understanding basic operators is an essential step. Operators in Python allow us to perform various operations on variables and values. They can be categorized into several types, including arithmetic, comparison, logical, and assignment operators. By exploring these groupings, we can uncover how Python uses symbols to manipulate data efficiently and accurately.

Let's start with the arithmetic operators, which are fundamental to performing mathematical operations. Python supports the basic arithmetic operations such as addition, subtraction, multiplication, division, and more. Here's a quick look at how these operations work:

1. **Addition (`+`)**: Used to add two numbers together.
   ```python
   x = 10
   y = 5
   result = x + y  # result is 15
   ```

2. **Subtraction (`-`)**: Used to subtract the second number from the first.
   ```python
   result = x - y  # result is 5
   ```

3. **Multiplication (`*`)**: Used to multiply two numbers.
   ```python
   result = x * y  # result is 50
   ```

4. **Division (`/`)**: Used to divide the first number by the second.

Important to note, division in Python results in a floating-point number.

```python
result = x / y  # result is 2.0
```

5. **Modulus (`%`)**: Returns the remainder when the first number is divided by the second.

```python
result = x % y  # result is 0
```

6. **Exponentiation (`**`)**: Raises the first number to the power of the second.

```python
result = x ** y  # result is 100000
```

7. **Floor Division (`//`)**: Divides the first number by the second, rounding down to the nearest integer.

```python
result = x // y  # result is 2
```

Moving on, comparison operators allow us to compare values and yield boolean results (`True` or `False`). Here's a brief overview:

1. **Equal (`==`)**: Checks if two values are equal.
   ```python
   result = (x == y)  # result is False
   ```

2. **Not Equal (`!=`)**: Checks if two values are not equal.
   ```python
   result = (x != y)  # result is True
   ```

3. **Greater Than (`>`)**: Checks if the first value is greater than the second.
   ```python
   result = (x > y)  # result is True
   ```

4. **Less Than (`<`)**: Checks if the first value is less than the second.
   ```python
   result = (x < y)  # result is False
   ```

5. **Greater Than or Equal To (`>=`)**: Checks if the first value is greater than or equal to the second.

   ```python
   result = (x >= y)  # result is True
   ```

6. **Less Than or Equal To (`<=`)**: Checks if the first value is less than or equal to the second.

   ```python
   result = (x <= y)  # result is False
   ```

Logical operators are also vital in Python, used primarily for combining conditional statements. They return boolean results based on the logical relationships of the conditions:

1. **Logical AND (`and`)**: Returns `True` if both conditions are `True`.

   ```python
   result = (x > 5 and y < 10)  # result is True
   ```

2. **Logical OR (`or`)**: Returns `True` if at least one of the

conditions is `True`.

```python
result = (x > 5 or y > 10)  # result is True
```

3. **Logical NOT (`not`)**: Reverses the result of the condition.

```python
result = not(x > 5)  # result is False
```

Lastly, understanding assignment operators helps us assign and update the values of variables in efficient ways. Apart from the basic assignment operator (`=`), Python offers several shorthand assignment operators for ease of use:

1. **Addition Assignment (`+=`)**:

```python
x += y  # equivalent to x = x + y
```

2. **Subtraction Assignment (`-=`)**:

```python
x -= y  # equivalent to x = x - y
```

3. **Multiplication Assignment (`*=`)**:

    ```python
    x *= y  # equivalent to x = x * y
    ```

4. **Division Assignment (`/=`)**:

    ```python
    x /= y  # equivalent to x = x / y
    ```

5. **Modulus Assignment (`%=`)**:

    ```python
    x %= y  # equivalent to x = x % y
    ```

6. **Exponentiation Assignment (`**=`)**:

    ```python
    x **= y  # equivalent to x = x ** y
    ```

7. **Floor Division Assignment (`//=`)**:

    ```python
    x //= y  # equivalent to x = x // y
    ```

```

Understanding and using these operators effectively will be foundational as we delve deeper into Python programming. Each operator contributes to the flexibility and power of Python as a language, enabling us to handle a wide range of programming tasks with ease and precision.

## Conditional Statements

Conditional statements are a fundamental aspect of many programming languages, including Python. They allow a program to execute certain blocks of code based on whether a specified condition is true or false. Think of conditional statements as a way to enable decision-making within your code; based on varying inputs or states, different outputs or actions can be generated.

Let's delve into how conditional statements work in Python:

### The `if` Statement

The most basic form of a conditional statement in Python is the `if` statement. It executes a block of code only if a specified condition evaluates to `True`.
```

```python
x = 10
if x > 5:
    print("x is greater than 5")
```

In this example, the condition `x > 5` is true, so the statement inside the `if` block is executed, resulting in the output: `x is greater than 5`.

The `else` Statement

What if you want to execute a different block of code when the condition is false? This is where the `else` statement comes in handy. It provides an alternative sequence of statements to execute if the initial `if` condition evaluates to `False`.

```python
x = 3
if x > 5:
    print("x is greater than 5")
else:
    print("x is 5 or less")
```

Since `x` is not greater than 5, the `else` block is executed and you'll see: `x is 5 or less`.

The `elif` Statement

Python also allows for multiple conditions to be checked with the `elif` (short for "else if") statement. This is useful when you have multiple conditions and want to execute different blocks of code based on which condition is true.

```python
x = 7
if x > 10:
    print("x is greater than 10")
elif x > 5:
    print("x is greater than 5 but less than or equal to 10")
else:
    print("x is 5 or less")
```

In this case, the condition `x > 5` is true, so the `elif` block gets executed, yielding: `x is greater than 5 but less than or equal to 10`.

Nested Conditionals

You can also nest conditional statements within each other. This means you can have an `if` statement inside another `if` or `else` block.

```python
x = 8
if x > 5:
    if x % 2 == 0:
        print("x is greater than 5 and even")
    else:
        print("x is greater than 5 and odd")
else:
    print("x is 5 or less")
```

Here, since `x` is greater than 5 and also even, the inner `if` block is executed, resulting in: `x is greater than 5 and even`.

Short-Circuiting

Python's conditional statements also support short-circuiting, which means that evaluation stops as soon as the result is known. This is particularly useful for conditions using logical operators like `and` and `or`.

```python
x = 8
y = 3
if x > 5 and y < 4:
    print("Both conditions are true")
```

In this example, since `x > 5` is true and `y < 4` is also true, the `if` block executes, resulting in: `Both conditions are true`.

Inline `if` Statements

For simple conditions, Python provides a more concise syntax known as the inline `if` or ternary conditional operator.

```python
x = 9
result = "x is even" if x % 2 == 0 else "x is odd"
print(result)
```

Here, `result` will be `"x is odd"` because the condition `x % 2 == 0` is false.

Understanding and effectively using conditional statements allows you to craft more dynamic and responsive programs. It is a critical skill for any Python programmer, serving as the foundation for more complex logic and decision-making in your code.

Loops

When you start learning Python, one of the fundamental concepts you'll encounter is loops. Loops are powerful programming constructs that allow you to execute a block of code multiple times, which is especially useful for tasks that involve repetitive actions. There are two primary types of loops in Python: `for` loops and `while` loops.

For Loops

The `for` loop is used to iterate over a sequence (like a list, tuple, dictionary, set, or string) and execute a block of code for each item in that sequence. Here's a basic example:

```python
fruits = ["apple", "banana", "cherry"]
for fruit in fruits:
    print(fruit)
```

```

In this example, the loop will print each fruit in the `fruits` list. The loop starts with the first element, "apple", and moves through the list one element at a time until it reaches the end.

One of the most common usages of the `for` loop is with the `range()` function, which generates a sequence of numbers. Here's how you can use it:

```python
for i in range(5):
    print(i)
```

This loop will print numbers from 0 to 4. The `range(5)` function generates a sequence of numbers starting from 0 up to (but not including) 5.

While Loops

`While` loops, on the other hand, continue to execute a block of code as long as a given condition is true. Here's an example:
```

```python
count = 0
while count < 5:
    print(count)
    count += 1
```

In this case, the loop will keep printing the value of `count` as long as `count` is less than 5. After each iteration, the value of `count` is incremented by 1. Once `count` reaches 5, the condition `count < 5` becomes false, and the loop terminates.

Breaking Out of Loops

There might be situations where you want to prematurely exit a loop. Python provides the `break` statement just for this purpose. Here's how you can use it:

```python
for i in range(10):
    if i == 5:
        break
    print(i)
```

In this example, the loop will print numbers from 0 to 4. Once `i` equals 5, the `break` statement is executed, terminating the loop.

Continuing a Loop

If you want to skip the rest of the current iteration and move on to the next one, you can use the `continue` statement. Here's an example:

```python
for i in range(10):
    if i % 2 == 0:
        continue
    print(i)
```

This loop will print only the odd numbers from 0 to 9. When `i` is even, the `continue` statement is executed, which skips the rest of the code inside the loop for that iteration and moves on to the next one.

Nested Loops

Python also supports nested loops, meaning you can have a loop inside another loop. Here's an example:

```python
for i in range(3):
    for j in range(3):
        print(f"i: {i}, j: {j}")
```

This will produce a grid of coordinates with `i` and `j` ranging from 0 to 2. Nested loops are useful for tasks like iterating over multi-dimensional data structures.

Looping Through a Dictionary

When dealing with dictionaries, you often need to loop through both keys and values. Here's how you can do it:

```python
person = {"name": "Alice", "age": 25, "city": "New York"}
for key, value in person.items():
    print(f"{key}: {value}")
```

This will iterate through the dictionary and print each key-value pair.

Conclusion

Loops are indispensable tools in Python programming. They help you automate repetitive tasks, making your code more efficient and readable. Understanding how to use `for` and `while` loops effectively, along with concepts like `break` and `continue`, will significantly enhance your ability to solve complex programming challenges. As you gain more experience, you'll find loops to be an integral part of your Python toolkit.

Comments

When you begin your journey with Python, one of the first tools you'll encounter are comments. Comments are like notes within your code; they provide context, explanations, reminders, or any other relevant information that can help you or others understand what the code is meant to do. They are not executed by Python, meaning they do not affect the outcome of your program, but they can significantly enhance its readability.

Python has a simple and intuitive syntax for comments. To create a single-line comment, you start the line with the hash symbol `#`. Anything that follows on that line will be ignored by the Python interpreter.

For example:

```python
# This is a single-line comment
print("Hello, world!")  # This comment is on the same line as the code
```

In the above example, the comment `# This is a single-line comment` is ignored by Python, as is `# This comment is on the same line as the code`. Only the `print("Hello, world!")` statement is executed.

If you need to write a longer comment that spans multiple lines, you have two main options. One is to use the `#` symbol at the beginning of each line:

```python
# This is a comment
# that spans multiple
# lines.
```

Another approach is to use multi-line strings, also known as docstrings, although technically they are not comments, they serve well for documentation:

```python
"""
```

This is a multi-line comment.

It can span multiple lines.
"""
```

However, keep in mind that while the multi-line string approach is often used to document functions and classes through docstrings, it is less commonly used purely for commenting in professional code.

Why are comments so important? Imagine coming back to your code after a few weeks, or someone else trying to understand it. Well-written comments can save a lot of time and confusion. They can describe the purpose of a function, the rationale behind a particular approach, or note where improvements are needed.

For instance, include comments to explain complex algorithms or the purpose of external libraries:

```python
# Using the requests library to fetch data from an API
import requests

response = requests.get('https://api.example.com/data')
data = response.json()

# Ensure data is valid
```
```

```
if 'error' in data:
    print("Error fetching data")
```

Sometimes, comments can also be used to mark tasks or vulnerabilities, often referred to as "to-do" comments:

```python
# TODO: Update API endpoint once the new version is available
# FIXME: Handle possible exceptions that may arise here
```

To conclude, commenting in Python (or any programming language) is an essential practice for writing maintainable, understandable, and collaborative code. Good comments do not over-explain the obvious but clarify the intent, purpose, and function of complex sections of code. They are a crucial element in the toolkit of any proficient programmer, aiding in both the development and debugging processes.

Indentation and Code Blocks

One of the hallmark features that often surprises new Python programmers is its reliance on indentation to define code blocks. Unlike many other programming languages that use braces or keywords to delineate code segments, Python uses indentation level to indicate the grouping of statements.

This fact can initially seem peculiar, especially if you are coming from a background in languages like C, Java, or JavaScript, where braces `{}` are commonly used to wrap code blocks. In Python, a block of code, such as the body of a function, loop, or conditional statement, starts after a colon (`:`) and continues with all the lines that are indented further than the starting line of that block.

Let's look at a simple example to illustrate this:

```python
if True:
    print("This is a block of code")
    print("Because it is indented")
print("This is outside the block")
```

In this example, the two `print` statements are part of the same block because they are indented to the same level after the `if True:` line. The string "This is outside the block" is not indented further, which signifies the end of the block associated with the `if` condition.

One of the advantages of this indentation-based syntax is that it inherently encourages code readability and neatly organized code structure. Indentation naturally breaks code into clear, manageable chunks that are easy to follow. However, it's crucial to be consistent with your use of tabs or spaces in a codebase. Python's style guide, PEP 8, recommends using 4 spaces per indentation level. Mixing tabs and spaces can lead to errors that are often subtle and hard to debug.

Consider a function definition as another example:

```python
def greet(name):
    print("Hello, " + name + "!")
    print("Welcome to Python programming.")
```

Here, both `print` statements are part of the `greet` function because they are indented with the same level. If you mistakenly align one of the `print` statements differently, Python will throw an `IndentationError`:

```python
def greet(name):
    print("Hello, " + name + "!")
```

```
    print("Welcome to Python programming.")
```

This code snippet will not run because the second `print` statement is not indented to the same level as the first one. Python will not understand that both statements are intended to be part of the `greet` function's body.

Many integrated development environments (IDEs) and text editors provide settings to automatically adjust indentation, but it's good practice to remain vigilant. Proper indentation is more than just an aesthetic choice in Python—it is a syntactic element essential for code execution.

In summary, Python's use of indentation for defining code blocks emphasizes the importance of writing clean, readable code. It may take some getting used to, but this clear and straightforward structuring simplifies understanding and maintaining code. Remember always to be consistent with your indentation, stick to the community's convention of using 4 spaces, and your code will be easier to read and less prone to subtle errors.

Basic Input and Output

When it comes to interacting with users, the two most fundamental operations you'll need to master in Python are input and output. These operations form the backbone of communication between your program and the user, allowing you to gather data and provide feedback or results.

Let's begin with the simplest form of output: using the `print()` function. The `print()` function is used to display information to the console, typically for the purpose of providing information to the user or debugging your code. Here's a very basic example:

```python
print("Hello, World!")
```

This command will output the text `Hello, World!` to the console. You can also use the `print()` function to display variables and more complex expressions. Consider the following example:

```python
name = "Alice"
age = 30
print("Name:", name)
print("Age:", age)
```

In this case, the `print()` function is used to display the value of the variables `name` and `age`. The output would be:

```
Name: Alice
Age: 30
```

Sometimes, you may want to format your output for readability. Python's f-strings (formatted string literals) are an excellent way to embed expressions inside string literals, using curly braces `{}`. Here's how you could use f-strings for the previous example:

```python
name = "Alice"
age = 30
print(f"Name: {name}")
print(f"Age: {age}")
```

This will produce the same result but in a more readable and concise manner.

Now, let's move on to the input aspect. To take input from the user, Python provides the `input()` function. When `input()` is called, the program will pause and wait for the user to type something and press Enter. Here's a simple example:

```python
name = input("Enter your name: ")
print(f"Hello, {name}!")
```

When you run this code, Python will display `Enter your name:`, wait for the user to input their name, and then greet the user using the name they typed. If the user types "Bob," for instance, the output will be:

```
Enter your name: Bob
Hello, Bob!
```

It's important to note that the `input()` function always returns a string. If you need to work with other data types (e.g., integers or floats), you will need to convert the input string to the desired type using type casting functions like `int()` or `float()`. Here's an example where we ask for a user's age:

```python
age = int(input("Enter your age: "))
print(f"You are {age} years old.")
```

In this code snippet, the user is prompted to enter their age. The input string is then converted to an integer using `int()`, and the result is printed.

Handling input and output effectively is essential for writing interactive programs. While it may seem basic, these fundamental skills are the building blocks for more complex operations and user interactions. As you become more comfortable with Python, you'll find that mastering these basics will enable you to create more dynamic and responsive applications.

Chapter 2: Data Structures

Lists

Lists are among the most versatile and widely used data structures in Python, providing a simple yet effective method for organizing related items. They are ordered collections that are mutable, meaning you can change their content even after they have been created.

At their core, lists are defined by enclosing a comma-separated sequence of items within square brackets, like so:

```python
fruits = ["apple", "banana", "cherry"]
```

Here, `fruits` is a list containing three string elements. Each item in a list is assigned a unique index, starting from zero. Thus, `fruits[0]` would access the first item, "apple".

Creating Lists

Creating a list is straightforward. You can either populate it with initial values or create an empty list and add items later:

```python
```

```
numbers = [1, 2, 3, 4, 5]
empty_list = []
```

Accessing Elements

As mentioned, you can access list items using their index. Negative indexing is also supported, where `-1` refers to the last item, `-2` to the second-to-last, and so on:

```python
first_fruit = fruits[0]    # "apple"
last_fruit = fruits[-1]    # "cherry"
```

Slicing Lists

Slicing allows you to access a range of items in a list. It's done by specifying a start and end index, separated by a colon:

```python
subset = fruits[1:3]    # ["banana", "cherry"]
```

Modifying Lists

Since lists are mutable, you can change their content. You can update a single element or a range of elements through slicing:

```python
fruits[1] = "blueberry"
fruits[0:2] = ["kiwi", "mango"]
```

Adding Elements

Adding elements to a list can be achieved using functions like `append()`, `insert()`, and `extend()`:

```python
fruits.append("grape")          # Adds to the end
fruits.insert(1, "orange")      # Inserts at index 1
fruits.extend(["pineapple", "pear"]) # Adds multiple elements
```

Removing Elements

Elements can be removed from a list in several ways, including using `remove()`, `pop()`, and `del`:

```python
fruits.remove("mango")        # Removes first occurrence of "mango"
popped_item = fruits.pop(2)   # Removes and returns the item at
```

index 2

del fruits[1]   # Deletes the item at index 1
```

### List Operations
Python lists support a variety of operations, such as concatenation and repetition, using the `+` and `*` operators, respectively:

```python
combined_list = fruits + numbers
repeated_fruits = fruits * 2
```

List Comprehensions
List comprehensions provide a concise way to create lists. It consists of brackets containing an expression followed by a `for` clause:

```python
squares = [x**2 for x in range(10)]  # [0, 1, 4, 9, 16, 25, 36, 49, 64, 81]
```

Membership Test
You can test if an item is in a list using the `in` keyword:
```

```python
"island" in fruits  # False
```

Built-in Functions

Several built-in functions and methods are handy for list manipulation. Common examples include `len()`, `min()`, `max()`, and `sort()`:

```python
length = len(fruits)       # Number of items in the list
minimum = min(numbers)     # Smallest element
numbers.sort()             # Sorts the list in ascending order
```

Lists in Python offer powerful capabilities for working with Sequential data, making them an essential tool for any Python programmer. Understanding how to leverage lists effectively will significantly enhance your coding proficiency.

Tuples

When we talk about data structures in Python, one of the most essential and versatile is the tuple. Tuples are a type of collection that allows you to group multiple items into a single structure. They are somewhat similar to lists but have some important key differences.

First and foremost, tuples are immutable. This means once a tuple is created, it cannot be modified. While you can create a new tuple based on existing ones, you can't change the elements of the original tuple. This feature makes tuples a great choice when you need a collection of items that should not change throughout the lifecycle of your program.

To create a tuple, you simply place the desired elements inside parentheses, separated by commas. Here's an example:

```python
my_tuple = (1, 2, 3, 4, 5)
```

Accessing the elements within a tuple is done via indexing, similar to lists. The index starts at 0, so `my_tuple[0]` would give you `1`, while `my_tuple[3]` would give you `4`.

This immutability brings about several advantages:

1. **Safety:** Because the contents of a tuple cannot be altered, you

can trust that the data you placed in a tuple stays constant throughout your program's execution. This can help avoid bugs that are caused by unintended changes to your data.

2. **Performance:** Tuples are generally faster than lists when it comes to iteration and accessing elements. This is because their immutability allows Python to optimize read-only access patterns.

3. **Dictionary Keys:** Because tuples are immutable, they can be used as keys in dictionaries, unlike lists. This is useful when you need a composite key—one that is made up of multiple components.

Here's an example demonstrating the use of a tuple as a dictionary key:

```python
location_data = {
    ("New York", "NY"): 8175133,
    ("Los Angeles", "CA"): 3792621,
    ("Chicago", "IL"): 2695598
}
```

In this case, each key is a tuple representing a city and state, and the associated value is the population of that city.

Despite their immutability, tuples can contain mutable objects, such as lists. For instance:

```python
mixed_tuple = (1, [2, 3], 4)
```

While you cannot alter the tuple itself (i.e., you can't add, remove, or change the immutable elements), you can still modify the mutable objects contained within. For instance, you could update the list inside `mixed_tuple`:

```python
mixed_tuple[1].append(4)
print(mixed_tuple)
```

This would output:

```
(1, [2, 3, 4], 4)
```

Tuples also support various built-in functions and methods. For example:

- `len()`: Returns the number of items in the tuple.
- `max()`, `min()`: Returns the maximum or minimum value.
- `sum()`: Returns the sum of items, if they are numbers.
- `tuple()`: This function can convert other collection types like lists into tuples.

Just as with lists, you can also use slicing to access a range of elements within the tuple:

```python
my_tuple = (0, 1, 2, 3, 4, 5)
print(my_tuple[1:4])  # Outputs: (1, 2, 3)
```

You can slice `[1:4]` to get elements starting from index `1` and stopping before index `4`.

There are some cases where you need to ensure a tuple rather than a single value. For instance, `(3)` represents a number, but `(3,)` represents a tuple with a single element. This distinction is crucial in cases where the tuple is required, and forgetting the comma would lead to an error.

In summary, tuples are a fundamental and powerful part of Python's data structure toolbox, providing a way to group related data together in a safe, predictable, and often efficient manner. Whether you need an immutable sequence of items or a composite key for a dictionary, tuples are the go-to structure. By understanding and leveraging their unique properties, you can write more robust and maintainable Python code.

Dictionaries

Imagine you have a collection of items, each associated with a unique label. In programming terms, this is essentially what a dictionary does. In Python, a dictionary is a versatile and highly efficient data structure that allows you to map keys to values. At its core, a dictionary is an unordered collection of items, but what sets it apart is its ability to handle key-value pairs.

Let's start with the basics. To create a dictionary in Python, you use curly braces `{}` and separate keys and values with colons. For example:

```python
```

```python
student_grades = {
    "Alice": 89,
    "Bob": 95,
    "Charlie": 78
}
```

In this dictionary, the keys are the names of the students ("Alice", "Bob", and "Charlie"), and the values are their respective grades.

Accessing Values

To access a value in a dictionary, you use the key associated with it. For instance, if you want to find out Bob's grade, you would write:

```python
bob_grade = student_grades["Bob"]
print(bob_grade)
```

This would output `95`.

Modifying Dictionaries

Dictionaries are mutable, meaning you can change them after creation. You could add a new student's grade like this:

```python
student_grades["David"] = 82
```

Or update an existing student's grade:

```python
student_grades["Alice"] = 91
```

Removing Items

Items can also be removed using the `del` keyword:

```python
del student_grades["Charlie"]
```

After this line of code runs, the dictionary would no longer contain an entry for "Charlie".

Checking for Keys

Before you access a value, it's often a good idea to check if a key exists to avoid KeyError. This can be done using the `in` keyword:

```python
if "Alice" in student_grades:
    print(student_grades["Alice"])
```

This code checks if "Alice" is a key in `student_grades` and prints her grade if she is.

Iterating Through a Dictionary

Dictionaries support various methods of iteration. You can iterate through the keys, the values, or both. Here's how you can print all the keys and values:

```python
for student in student_grades:
    print(f"{student}: {student_grades[student]}")
```

Or, using the `items()` method to directly access keys and their corresponding values:

```python
for student, grade in student_grades.items():
    print(f"{student}: {grade}")
```

Dictionary Methods

Python dictionaries come with a set of built-in methods that can be incredibly useful. Here's a quick look at a few of them:

- `clear()`: Removes all items from the dictionary.
  ```python
  student_grades.clear()
  ```

- `keys()`: Returns a view object of all the keys.
  ```python
  print(student_grades.keys())
  ```

- `values()`: Returns a view object of all the values.

```python
print(student_grades.values())
```

- `get(key, default_value)`: Returns the value for a key, or a default value if the key is not found.
```python
print(student_grades.get("Eve", 0))
```

Nested Dictionaries

In more complex scenarios, you might find yourself needing to store dictionaries within dictionaries. This is particularly useful for representing structured data. For instance:

```python
students = {
    "Alice": {"grade": 89, "age": 20},
    "Bob": {"grade": 95, "age": 22},
    "Charlie": {"grade": 78, "age": 21}
}
```

You can access nested values by chaining square brackets:

```python
alice_grade = students["Alice"]["grade"]
print(alice_grade)
```

This would output `89`.

Conclusion

Dictionaries are powerful tools in Python that offer a lot of flexibility and functionality. They are ideal for scenarios where you need a logical association between a key and a value, such as mappings, data representation, and more. Their ability to dynamically adjust and their straightforward syntax make them an indispensable part of the Python programmer's toolkit.

Sets

When you think about storing unique items, your mind might drift towards a variety of data structures, but one of the most robust and efficient ways you can do this in Python is using a set. Sets are a powerful tool in Python that allows you to store unordered collections of unique items. Unlike lists or tuples, sets do not allow duplicates, making them ideal for operations that require each item to be distinct.

Creating a Set

To create a set in Python, you can use curly braces `{}` or the built-in `set()` function. Here's a simple example:

```python
# Using curly braces
my_set = {1, 2, 3, 4}
print(my_set)

# Using the set() function
another_set = set([1, 2, 3, 4])
print(another_set)
```

Both of these will result in sets containing the numbers 1, 2, 3, and 4. It's important to note that even if you try to add duplicates to a set, Python will automatically handle them for you:

```python
dup_set = {1, 2, 2, 3, 4, 4, 4}
print(dup_set)
```

```

The output here will be `{1, 2, 3, 4}`, as sets do not allow duplicates.

### Adding and Removing Elements

You can always add or remove elements from a set using the `add()` and `remove()` methods respectively:

```python
my_set = {1, 2, 3}
print(my_set)

my_set.add(4)
print(my_set)

my_set.remove(2)
print(my_set)
```

Set Operations

One of the key strengths of sets is their ability to perform mathematical set operations like union, intersection, difference, and
```

symmetric difference. These operations allow you to handle complex data manipulations effortlessly.

1. **Union** - Combines elements from both sets, removing duplicates:

```python
set1 = {1, 2, 3}
set2 = {3, 4, 5}
union_set = set1.union(set2)
print(union_set) # Output: {1, 2, 3, 4, 5}
```

2. **Intersection** - Returns elements that are common to both sets:

```python
set1 = {1, 2, 3}
set2 = {2, 3, 4}
intersection_set = set1.intersection(set2)
print(intersection_set) # Output: {2, 3}
```

3. **Difference** - Returns elements that are in the first set but not in the second:

```python
set1 = {1, 2, 3}
set2 = {2, 3, 4}
difference_set = set1.difference(set2)
print(difference_set)  # Output: {1}
```

4. **Symmetric Difference** - Returns elements that are in either of the sets, but not in both:

```python
set1 = {1, 2, 3}
set2 = {2, 3, 4}
sym_diff_set = set1.symmetric_difference(set2)
print(sym_diff_set)  # Output: {1, 4}
```

Practical Uses

Sets can be particularly useful in scenarios like removing duplicates from a list, performing membership tests, and handling complex data manipulations.

For example, if you have a list of email addresses and you want to make sure each is unique, converting the list to a set will do the job efficiently:

```python
email_list = ["test@example.com", "hello@example.com", "test@example.com"]
unique_emails = set(email_list)
print(unique_emails)   # Output: {'test@example.com', 'hello@example.com'}
```

Additionally, sets are incredibly fast for membership tests, i.e., checking if an element is in the set:

```python
letters = {'a', 'b', 'c'}
print('a' in letters)  # Output: True
print('d' in letters)  # Output: False
```

This can be particularly valuable when dealing with large datasets, providing an efficient way to handle lookups.

Conclusion

Sets bring a lot of power and flexibility to the table when dealing with unique collections of items in Python. With efficient operations for union, intersection, and other mathematical functions, sets can help streamline data manipulation and reduce complexity in your code. By understanding how to effectively use sets, you'll be better equipped to handle a variety of programming challenges with elegance and efficiency.

String Manipulation

When diving into the world of Python programming, one of the foundational skills you'll need to master is string manipulation. Strings are a crucial data type in Python, serving as a means to represent text and characters, and the ways in which you can manipulate these strings provide powerful tools for solving a myriad of programming problems.

One of the simplest and most common operations you'll perform on strings is concatenation. In Python, you can concatenate, or join, strings together using the `+` operator. For instance:

```python
greeting = "Hello"
```

```
name = "World"
message = greeting + ", " + name + "!"
print(message)
```

This would output:

```
Hello, World!
```

In addition to concatenation, Python offers a wealth of other string manipulation tools. Let's explore a few:

Slicing and Indexing
Strings are sequences of characters, and you can access individual characters using indexing. Python uses zero-based indexing, so the first character of a string `s` is `s[0]`, the second character is `s[1]`, and so on. Here's an example:

```python
text = "Python"
print(text[0])  # Outputs: P
print(text[2])  # Outputs: t
```

```

Moreover, you can extract sub-strings using slicing. The syntax for slicing is `s[start:end]`, where `start` is the beginning index and `end` is the ending index but not inclusive:

```python
print(text[1:4])  # Outputs: yth
```

If you omit the starting index, slicing starts from the beginning of the string. Likewise, if you omit the ending index, slicing goes on till the end of the string:

```python
print(text[:2])  # Outputs: Py
print(text[3:])  # Outputs: hon
```

String Methods

Python strings come with a variety of built-in methods that make string manipulation straightforward. Here are some commonly used methods:
```

- `upper()`: Converts all characters in a string to uppercase.
- `lower()`: Converts all characters in a string to lowercase.
- `strip()`: Removes any leading and trailing whitespaces.
- `replace()`: Replaces a specified phrase with another specified phrase.
- `split()`: Splits a string into a list where each word is a list item.

Examples:

```python
sentence = " Hello, Python! "
print(sentence.upper())    # Outputs:  HELLO, PYTHON!
print(sentence.lower())    # Outputs:  hello, python!
print(sentence.strip())    # Outputs: Hello, Python!
print(sentence.replace("Python", "World")) # Outputs:  Hello, World!
print(sentence.split())    # Outputs: ['Hello,', 'Python!']
```

f-Strings
Introduced in Python 3.6, f-strings (formatted string literals) provide a way to embed expressions inside string literals, using curly braces `{}`. They are prefixed with `f` and allow for inline evaluations:

```python
```

```
name = "Python"
version = 3.8
formatted_string = f"{name} version {version}"
print(formatted_string)  # Outputs: Python version 3.8
```

Regular Expressions

For more advanced string manipulation tasks, Python's `re` module allows the use of regular expressions. Regular expressions are a powerful way to search, match, and manipulate strings based on patterns. Here's an example that finds all occurrences of the word "Python" in a text:

```python
import re

text = "Python is versatile. Python can be used for web development, data analysis, and more."
matches = re.findall(r"Python", text)
print(matches)  # Outputs: ['Python', 'Python']
```

Regular expressions can be complex but incredibly useful for text parsing and validation.

Mastering string manipulation is fundamental for any Python programmer. The more you practice, the more proficient you'll become at using these tools to handle and transform strings effectively. Whether you're cleaning data, parsing text, or generating dynamic output, your ability to manipulate strings will play a pivotal role in your success as a coder.

List Comprehensions

List comprehensions are a concise way to create lists in Python. They're often more readable and expressive than using traditional loops and appending elements one by one. Let's dive into what list comprehensions are and how to use them effectively.

Basic Syntax

A list comprehension consists of brackets containing an expression followed by a `for` clause. The simplest form looks like this:

```python
[expression for item in iterable]
```

For example, imagine you want to create a list of squares for numbers 0 through 9. Using a traditional loop, this might look like:

```python
squares = []
for x in range(10):
    squares.append(x**2)
```

With a list comprehension, you can achieve the same result in a single line of code:

```python
squares = [x**2 for x in range(10)]
```

This not only reduces the amount of code, but it also makes your intent clearer to someone reading your code.

Adding Conditions

You can add a condition to a list comprehension to filter items from the original iterable. To add a conditional clause, use the following format:

```python
[expression for item in iterable if condition]
```

Let's say you only want the squares of even numbers. You could modify our previous example like so:

```python
even_squares = [x**2 for x in range(10) if x % 2 == 0]
```

Here, `x % 2 == 0` is the condition that filters out odd numbers, so the resulting list contains only the squares of even numbers.

Nested List Comprehensions

List comprehensions can also be nested. This is particularly useful when working with multi-dimensional data structures like matrices. The nested list comprehension format is:

```python
[expression for item1 in iterable1 for item2 in iterable2]
```

For instance, if you want to flatten a 2D list (a list of lists), you could use nested comprehensions:

```python
matrix = [[1, 2, 3], [4, 5, 6], [7, 8, 9]]
flattened = [num for row in matrix for num in row]
```

In this example, `row` goes through each sublist within `matrix`, and then `num` picks each element within those sublists, effectively flattening the 2D list into a 1D list.

List Comprehensions vs. Loop Constructs

While list comprehensions offer a more compact and readable syntax for creating lists, there are cases where traditional loops are more appropriate. For example, if the logic within your loop becomes too complex, a list comprehension might reduce readability rather than enhance it. In such cases, stick to using traditional loops where the intent and logic are clear.

Example Scenarios

Here are some practical scenarios where list comprehensions can be particularly useful:

1. **Transforming Data**: Convert a list of strings to lowercase:
   ```python
   fruits = ["Apple", "Banana", "Cherry"]
   lowercase_fruits = [fruit.lower() for fruit in fruits]
   ```

2. **Extracting Important Information**: Extracting the first letter from each word:
   ```python
   words = ["hello", "world", "python"]
   first_letters = [word[0] for word in words]
   ```

3. **Conditional Logic**: Filtering out negative numbers from a list:
   ```python
   numbers = [-3, -2, -1, 0, 1, 2, 3]
   positive_numbers = [num for num in numbers if num > 0]
   ```

4. **Generating Combinations**: Creating a Cartesian product of two lists:
   ```python
   ```

```
colors = ['red', 'blue']
sizes = ['S', 'M', 'L']
cartesian_product = [(color, size) for color in colors for size in sizes]
```

Conclusion

List comprehensions are a powerful feature in Python that allow for more readable and concise code. They're particularly useful for simple transformations and data filtering tasks. However, it's essential to strike a balance between clarity and brevity. Use them wisely to improve the readability and efficiency of your code.

Dictionary Comprehensions

Dictionary comprehensions are one of the more elegant and expressive features in Python, allowing you to create dictionaries in a succinct and readable manner. Just as list comprehensions provide a compact way to create lists, dictionary comprehensions allow you to construct dictionaries more effortlessly. Understanding how to use them effectively can greatly enhance your coding efficiency and readability.

The Basic Syntax

The basic syntax for a dictionary comprehension is quite similar to that of a list comprehension. The standard format looks like this:

```python
{key_expression: value_expression for item in iterable if condition}
```

Let's break it down:
- `key_expression`: This is the expression that determines the keys of the new dictionary.
- `value_expression`: This expression defines the values associated with the keys.
- `for item in iterable`: This part iterates over each item in the iterable.
- `if condition`: This is an optional clause to filter items.

Here's a simple example to get you started:

```python
squares = {x: x*x for x in range(6)}
print(squares)
```

In this example, the code creates a dictionary where the keys are numbers from 0 to 5 and the values are the squares of the keys. The output will be:

```python
{0: 0, 1: 1, 2: 4, 3: 9, 4: 16, 5: 25}
```

Adding Conditions

Much like list comprehensions, dictionary comprehensions can also include conditional logic. This allows you to filter the items in the iterable before they are added to the dictionary. For instance:

```python
even_squares = {x: x*x for x in range(10) if x % 2 == 0}
print(even_squares)
```

Here, the dictionary comprehension filters out odd numbers, creating a dictionary only for even numbers. The output will be:

```python
{0: 0, 2: 4, 4: 16, 6: 36, 8: 64}
```

Using Functions in Dictionary Comprehensions

You can also use functions within dictionary comprehensions, making them more dynamic and powerful. Consider the following example:

```python
def cube(x):
    return x*x*x

cubes = {x: cube(x) for x in range(6)}
print(cubes)
```

In this snippet, we define a function `cube` that returns the cube of a number and then use it in the dictionary comprehension to generate a dictionary of cubes:

```python
{0: 0, 1: 1, 2: 8, 3: 27, 4: 64, 5: 125}
```

Nested Dictionary Comprehensions

Sometimes, you may find yourself needing to create a dictionary where the values are themselves dictionaries. You can achieve this with nested comprehensions. Here's an example:

```python
nested_dict = {x: {y: x*y for y in range(5)} for x in range(3)}
print(nested_dict)
```

This code creates a dictionary where each value is another dictionary containing products of the keys. The output will be:

```python
{
    0: {0: 0, 1: 0, 2: 0, 3: 0, 4: 0},
    1: {0: 0, 1: 1, 2: 2, 3: 3, 4: 4},
    2: {0: 0, 1: 2, 2: 4, 3: 6, 4: 8}
}
```

Practical Applications

Dictionary comprehensions can be incredibly useful for various practical applications, such as mapping data from one form to another or creating lookup tables. Here's an example that demonstrates how you might use it to build a dictionary mapping words to their lengths:

```python
words = ['apple', 'banana', 'cherry']
word_length = {word: len(word) for word in words}
print(word_length)
```

The output will be:
```python
{'apple': 5, 'banana': 6, 'cherry': 6}
```

Conclusion

Dictionary comprehensions are a powerful tool in Python, enabling you to create and manipulate dictionaries with minimal code. They promote cleaner, more readable, and more efficient code, making them a must-know technique for any Python programmer.

Chapter 3: Functions and Modules

Defining and Calling Functions

In any programming language, functions serve as the foundation for reusability and organization. By encapsulating code into individual, named blocks, functions allow us to write cleaner, more manageable, and more modular code. In Python, defining and calling functions is straightforward, making it an ideal starting point for beginners.

Defining a Function

To define a function in Python, you use the `def` keyword, followed by the function name and parentheses `()`. Inside the parentheses, you can specify parameters—these are the variables that will receive input values when the function is called. After closing the parentheses, you end the line with a colon `:`. The subsequent lines are indented, forming the body of the function. Here's a simple example:

```python
def greet():
    print("Hello, World!")
```

```

In this example, we've defined a function named `greet` that prints "Hello, World!" to the console. Notice the indentation, which is crucial in Python for defining the scope of the function.

### Calling a Function

Once a function is defined, you can call it by simply writing its name followed by parentheses. Using the `greet` function we just defined, here's how you would call it:

```python
greet()
```

This would output:

```
Hello, World!
```

Functions with Parameters
```

Functions become more powerful with parameters. Parameters act as placeholders for the values that you pass into the function. Here's an example with parameters:

```python
def greet_person(name):
    print(f"Hello, {name}!")
```

In this function, `name` is a parameter. When you call this function, you pass an argument (a value) for the parameter:

```python
greet_person("Alice")
```

This will output:

```
Hello, Alice!
```

Returning Values

Sometimes, you'll want a function to send a value back to the part of the program that called it. This is done with the `return` statement. Here's a simple example:

```python
def add(a, b):
    return a + b
```

This function takes two parameters, `a` and `b`, and returns their sum. Now, you can call the function and store the result in a variable:

```python
result = add(3, 5)
print(result)
```

This will output:

```
8
```

Default Parameter Values

Python functions allow default parameter values, providing flexibility in function calls. If an argument isn't provided, the default value is used. Here's an example:

```python
def greet(name="Guest"):
    print(f"Hello, {name}!")
```

You can call this function with or without an argument:

```python
greet("Bob")
greet()
```

The first call will output:

```
Hello, Bob!
```

The second call will use the default value:

```
Hello, Guest!
```

Keyword Arguments

Functions in Python can also be called using keyword arguments, where you explicitly specify the value of each parameter by name. This enhances readability and reduces the risk of errors. Here's an example:

```python
def describe_pet(pet_name, animal_type="dog"):
    print(f"I have a {animal_type} named {pet_name}.")
```

This function can be called like so:

```python
describe_pet("Whiskers", "cat")
describe_pet(pet_name="Buddy")
describe_pet(animal_type="hamster", pet_name="Nibbles")
```

The outputs will be:

```
I have a cat named Whiskers.
I have a dog named Buddy.
I have a hamster named Nibbles.
```

Summary

Defining and calling functions in Python is a fundamental skill that can greatly improve the efficiency and readability of your code. With an understanding of basic function syntax, parameters, return values, default arguments, and keyword arguments, you're well on your way to creating more modular and reusable code. Functions are the workhorses of programming, making tasks more manageable and your programs more elegant.

Function Arguments

When it comes to functions in Python, understanding how to use function arguments effectively is critical. Function arguments are the variables that we pass into a function, allowing for its operation to be dynamic and flexible.

Positional Arguments

Positional arguments are the simplest form. They are passed into the function in the order they are defined. Let's look at a simple example to illustrate this:

```python
def greet(first_name, last_name):
    print(f"Hello, {first_name} {last_name}!")

greet("Jane", "Doe")
```

In this example, "Jane" is assigned to `first_name` and "Doe" to `last_name` based on their positions. This is easy and straightforward for functions with a small number of parameters, but it can become confusing when dealing with more parameters.

Keyword Arguments

Keyword arguments, or named arguments, allow you to specify which argument corresponds to which parameter, regardless of their order.

```python
greet(last_name="Smith", first_name="John")
```

```

This format clarifies which value corresponds to which parameter, enhancing readability and reducing the potential for errors, especially in functions with multiple parameters.

### Default Values
Sometimes, you might want to provide default values to parameters. Default values are specified in the function definition and are used if no corresponding argument is passed when the function is called.

```python
def greet(first_name, last_name="Smith"):
    print(f"Hello, {first_name} {last_name}!")

greet("Joe")
```

If called with only one argument, the function uses the default value "Smith" for `last_name`. However, if both arguments are provided, the default value is overridden.

Variable-Length Arguments
Python allows functions to receive an arbitrary number of arguments
```

using the `*args` and `**kwargs` syntax.

*args
The `*args` parameter allows for handling a variable number of positional arguments.

```python
def greet(*names):
    for name in names:
        print(f"Hello, {name}!")

greet("Alice", "Bob", "Charlie")
```

In this instance, `*names` captures all additional positional arguments as a tuple.

**kwargs
The `**kwargs` parameter allows for handling a variable number of keyword arguments.

```python
def greet(**name_details):
    for key, value in name_details.items():
```

```
    print(f"{key.capitalize()}: {value}")

greet(first_name="Carol", last_name="Danvers", age=35)
```

Here, `**name_details` captures all keyword arguments as a dictionary, enabling even more flexibility.

Mixing Different Argument Types
Python also supports functions that use a mix of positional, keyword, and variable-length arguments. However, there are rules regarding the order in which these must be defined.

1. Standard positional arguments
2. *args
3. Keyword arguments
4. **kwargs

```python
def greet(greeting, *names, punctuation="!"):
    for name in names:
        print(f"{greeting}, {name}{punctuation}")

greet("Hi", "Alice", "Bob", punctuation=".")
```

```

This mix ensures that your function can be as flexible and intuitive as needed.

### Conclusion

Understanding how to utilize function arguments effectively can vastly improve the flexibility, readability, and maintainability of your Python code. By mastering positional arguments, keyword arguments, default values, and variable-length arguments, you'll be well-equipped to write more dynamic and robust functions.

# Return Statement

Functions in Python are versatile and pivotal elements in programming, acting as building blocks for larger applications. Among the many components that make up a function, the return statement holds particular significance. Understanding its role and functionality is crucial for both beginners and seasoned developers.

The return statement serves as the exit point of a function. When the return statement is encountered, the function exits, and the specified value is sent back to the caller. If no return statement is provided, the function returns `None` by default. This makes it clear that functions can be designed to either return a useful value or merely perform a
```

task.

Consider a simple function that adds two numbers:

```python
def add_numbers(a, b):
    result = a + b
    return result
```

In this example, the `return result` line sends the computed sum back to where the function was called. If you were to invoke this function, you could capture and utilize the returned value like so:

```python
sum = add_numbers(5, 3)
print(sum)  # Outputs: 8
```

This ability to return values is particularly useful when designing more complex functions. A function can perform calculations, process input, or manipulate data, and then provide the caller with the outcome.

Moreover, a function in Python is not limited to returning just one value. Using tuples, lists, or dictionaries, multiple values can be returned if needed:

```python
def calculate(a, b):
    sum_result = a + b
    difference = a - b
    return sum_result, difference

result_sum, result_diff = calculate(10, 5)
print(result_sum) # Outputs: 15
print(result_diff) # Outputs: 5
```

In the above snippet, `calculate` returns a tuple containing both the sum and the difference of the two numbers. When calling this function, Python smartly unpacks the tuple into separate variables.

Another critical point to consider is the immediacy of the return statement. Once a return statement is executed, the function stops running any further code. This behavior allows functions to manage logic elegantly:

```python
def check_even_odd(number):
    if number % 2 == 0:
        return 'Even'
    return 'Odd'
```

Here, the function checks if a number is even. If the condition is met, it returns 'Even' and exits. If not, the function proceeds to return 'Odd'.

You may also encounter scenarios where multiple return statements appear within the same function. This often occurs in functions with diverse operational paths based on conditions:

```python
def grade(score):
    if score >= 90:
        return 'A'
    elif score >= 80:
        return 'B'
    elif score >= 70:
        return 'C'
    elif score >= 60:
```

```
        return 'D'
    else:
        return 'F'
```

In this grading example, the function evaluates the score and returns the corresponding letter grade. Each return statement provides a different outcome based on the input score, ensuring that the correct grade is provided without further unnecessary evaluation.

It's worth noting that return statements can also return nothing, effectively ending the function and providing `None` as the result. Although seemingly trivial, this behavior is useful in certain design patterns or when the function's purpose doesn't require a return value.

Understanding the return statement and its implications enhances one's ability to write more effective and readable Python code. By leveraging this powerful feature, functions can become more flexible, organized, and informative, leading to better overall software design.

Lambda Functions

Lambda functions in Python, often referred to as anonymous functions, are small, unnamed functions defined using the `lambda` keyword. These functions are typically used for creating quick, throwaway functions that are not reused later in the code.

Basic Syntax and Usage

The syntax for a lambda function is straightforward:
```python
lambda arguments: expression
```

Here, `arguments` are the input parameters, and `expression` is the single expression that is evaluated and returned. Unlike regular functions defined with the `def` keyword, lambda functions are limited to a single expression. However, this doesn't mean they lack power. Here's a simple example to illustrate:
```python
double = lambda x: x * 2
print(double(5))  # Output: 10
```

In the above example, `lambda x: x * 2` is a lambda function that takes one argument (`x`) and returns `x` multiplied by 2.

Use Cases for Lambda Functions

1. **Quick Utility Functions**: Lambda functions are especially useful when you need a small utility function for short-term use. For instance, you might need a simple function to use with higher-order functions such as `map()`, `filter()`, or `sorted()`.

2. **Callables in GUI Programming**: In GUI programming, lambda functions can be used to define simple callbacks or event handlers.

3. **Inline Function Definitions**: Sometimes you need a function that is used only once or needs to be passed immediately as an argument. Lambda functions serve this purpose well without the need for formally defining a function with the `def` keyword.

Examples with Higher-Order Functions

Lambda functions shine when used with functions like `map()`, `filter()`, and `sorted()`. These higher-order functions take another function as an argument and apply it to a sequence or collection of items.

- **Using `map()`**:
  ```python
  numbers = [1, 2, 3, 4, 5]
  ```

```python
squares = list(map(lambda x: x**2, numbers))
print(squares)  # Output: [1, 4, 9, 16, 25]
```

Here, `lambda x: x**2` is used to square each number in the `numbers` list.

- **Using `filter()`**:
  ```python
  numbers = [1, 2, 3, 4, 5, 6]
  even_numbers = list(filter(lambda x: x % 2 == 0, numbers))
  print(even_numbers)  # Output: [2, 4, 6]
  ```

The lambda function `lambda x: x % 2 == 0` filters out the even numbers from the `numbers` list.

- **Using `sorted()`**:
  ```python
  words = ['python', 'lambda', 'functions', 'are', 'cool']
  sorted_words = sorted(words, key=lambda x: len(x))
  print(sorted_words)   # Output: ['are', 'cool', 'python', 'lambda', 'functions']
  ```

In this example, `lambda x: len(x)` sorts the list of words by their length.

Limitations and Considerations

While lambda functions are powerful, they come with certain limitations:

1. **Single Expression Only**: Lambda functions can only contain a single expression. This limits their complexity but also ensures they remain concise and readable.

2. **Reduced Readability**: Overusing lambda functions, especially in complex code, can make the code harder to read. In such cases, defining a regular function with the `def` keyword is preferable.

3. **Lack of Documentation**: Unlike regular functions, lambda functions cannot have a docstring, making it harder to document their purpose and usage.

Conclusion

Lambda functions are a concise and versatile feature in Python. They are particularly useful for short, throwaway functions and can significantly simplify code when used with higher-order functions. However, it's essential to strike a balance and not overuse lambda functions at the expense of code readability and maintainability.

Importing Modules

When you start writing larger Python programs, you'll soon realize that some tasks recur in different parts of your code. Instead of rewriting the same piece of code multiple times, you can use modules to compartmentalize and reuse functionality. In Python, a module is simply a file containing Python definitions and statements.

Python comes with a rich ecosystem of modules. Some of these are built into Python, while others can be installed from external sources. By importing these modules, you can tap into an extensive library of pre-written code, simplifying your programming efforts significantly.

The `import` Statement

The most straightforward way to include a module in your program is by using the `import` statement. This statement allows you to bring in the entire module, making all its functions and classes available for use.

```python
import math
```

After importing the `math` module, you can use its various functions and constants like so:

```python
import math

print(math.pi)      # Output: 3.141592653589793
print(math.sqrt(16)) # Output: 4.0
```

Here, `math.pi` and `math.sqrt` are accessed through the `math` module namespace, preventing any potential naming conflicts with other parts of your code.

Importing Specific Functions or Variables

If you only need a few functions or variables from a module, you can import them directly. This can make your code more concise and readable.

```python
from math import pi, sqrt

print(pi)        # Output: 3.141592653589793
print(sqrt(16))  # Output: 4.0
```

Renaming Imports

Sometimes module names can be long, and typing them repeatedly can be cumbersome. Python allows you to rename modules using the `as` keyword for ease of use.

```python
import numpy as np

# Now you can use np instead of numpy
array = np.array([1, 2, 3])
print(array)
```

Importing Everything

Python also provides a way to import everything from a module at once using the `*` operator. However, this is generally discouraged because it can lead to unintended interactions inside your namespace.

```python
from math import *

print(pi)      # Output: 3.141592653589793
print(sin(0))  # Output: 0.0
```

Checking Available Modules

To see which modules are available in your Python environment, you can use the `help()` function in an interactive Python session:

```python
help('modules')
```

This will provide a list of all available modules you can import and use.

Custom Modules

The true power of modules is realized when you create your own. Suppose you have common functions you use in multiple scripts. Place them in a file named, let's say `mymodule.py`:

```python
# mymodule.py
def greeting(name):
    return f"Hello, {name}!"
```

Now, you can import this custom module into another script:

```python
import mymodule

print(mymodule.greeting('Alice'))  # Output: Hello, Alice!
```

Creating custom modules not only keeps your code organized but also promotes reusability and maintainability.

Import Path

Python looks for modules in certain places, which are listed in `sys.path`. This list usually contains the current directory, various installation-specific directories, and `site-packages`. You can modify `sys.path` to include directories where your custom modules are located:

```python
import sys
sys.path.append('/path/to/your/module')
```

Conclusion

Modules are the backbone of organizing code in Python, making it more modular, reusable, and manageable. Whether using built-in modules, installing them from external sources, or creating your own, mastering the `import` mechanism is essential for any Python programmer. Keep experimenting with modules to see how they can simplify your coding life and open up new possibilities in your programming journey.

Standard Library Modules

Python's standard library is a treasure trove of modules that simplify many common programming tasks. These modules are part of the

Python distribution and can be used right out of the box without requiring any additional installation. Let's explore some of the most essential and frequently used modules in the standard library.

The `math` Module

For anyone dealing with mathematics, the `math` module is indispensable. It provides a wide array of mathematical functions, including trigonometric, logarithmic, and exponential functions.

```python
import math

print(math.sqrt(16))         # Output: 4.0
print(math.pi)               # Output: 3.141592653589793
print(math.sin(math.pi / 2)) # Output: 1.0
```

Whether you're handling simple arithmetic or complex calculations, the `math` module proves to be immensely valuable.

The `datetime` Module

Time and date manipulation are common in many applications, and

Python's `datetime` module makes it both straightforward and powerful.

```python
import datetime

now = datetime.datetime.now()
print("Current date and time: ", now)            # Output: Current date and time: 2023-10-15 14:21:30.730373
print("Today's date: ", now.date())              # Output: Today's date: 2023-10-15
print("Current year: ", now.year)                # Output: Current year: 2023
print("Current month: ", now.month)              # Output: Current month: 10
print("Current day: ", now.day)                  # Output: Current day: 15

custom_date = datetime.datetime(2023, 10, 15, 14, 45, 0)
print("Custom date and time: ", custom_date)     # Output: Custom date and time: 2023-10-15 14:45:00
```

With the `datetime` module, date and time calculations, formatting, and even timezone manipulations are effortlessly handled.

The `os` and `sys` Modules

Interacting with the operating system and the current Python runtime environment often requires the use of the `os` and `sys` modules.

The `os` module lets you perform a wide range of operating system operations such as file and directory manipulation.

```python
import os

print(os.name)              # Output: posix (on Unix-like systems) or nt (on Windows)
print(os.getcwd())          # Output: Current working directory

os.mkdir('new_directory')   # Creates a new directory
os.chdir('new_directory')   # Changes the current working directory to 'new_directory'
print(os.getcwd())          # Output: /current/path/new_directory
```

The `sys` module provides access to variables and functions related to the Python runtime environment.

```python
import sys

print(sys.version)            # Output: Python version info
print(sys.executable)         # Output: Path to the Python interpreter executable

if len(sys.argv) > 1:
    print("Command line arguments: ", sys.argv)  # Output: List of command line arguments
```

These modules are incredibly useful for system-level scripting and automation tasks.

The `random` Module

For all things random, the `random` module is your go-to resource. It generates pseudo-random numbers for simulations, games, or any application requiring randomization.

```python
```

```
import random

print(random.randint(1, 10))        # Output: Random integer between 1 and 10
print(random.random())              # Output: Random float between 0.0 and 1.0
print(random.choice(['apple', 'banana', 'cherry']))    # Output: Randomly-selected fruit

# Shuffle a list
my_list = [1, 2, 3, 4, 5]
random.shuffle(my_list)
print(my_list)                      # Output: The original list, shuffled randomly
```

The `random` module makes it easy to deal with randomness, whether you need random integers, floats, choices from a list, or even a shuffled list.

The `json` Module

In today's world of web services and APIs, the `json` module is becoming increasingly important. It allows for easy parsing and generation of JSON (JavaScript Object Notation) data.

```python
import json

# JSON encoding
data = {'name': 'John', 'age': 30, 'city': 'New York'}
json_string = json.dumps(data)
print(json_string)  # Output: {"name": "John", "age": 30, "city": "New York"}

# JSON decoding
decoded_data = json.loads(json_string)
print(decoded_data)  # Output: {'name': 'John', 'age': 30, 'city': 'New York'}
print(decoded_data['name'])  # Output: John
```

The `json` module seamlessly handles conversions between JSON and Python dictionaries, making API integrations considerably easier.

These examples only scratch the surface of Python's standard library, but they should give you a good starting point. Each of these modules is well-documented and supported, making them reliable tools in your Python programming toolkit.

Creating Your Own Modules

When you first embark on your Python journey, you'll often find yourself writing code in a single script file. This is perfectly fine for small projects or simple tasks, but as your projects grow in complexity, managing your code in one file becomes increasingly cumbersome. This is where modules come into play. Modules are Python files that contain function definitions, variables, and classes which you can import into other Python files in your project. In this subchapter, you'll learn how to create your own modules, making your code more modular, reusable, and maintainable.

Why Use Modules?

Modules help you to partition your code into manageable, logical sections. They promote code reuse because once a module is written and tested, it can be reused across multiple programs. Additionally, modules simplify maintenance; if a bug is found or an improvement is made in a module, you only have to update the code in one place.

Creating Your Own Module

Creating a module in Python is straightforward. Essentially, a module is just a Python file with a `.py` extension that contains functions, variables, and classes. Let's walk through an example to understand this better.

Step-by-Step Example

Suppose you are working on a simple math utility. You could create a file named `mymath.py` with the following content:

```python
# mymath.py

def add(a, b):
    return a + b

def subtract(a, b):
    return a - b

def multiply(a, b):
    return a * b

def divide(a, b):
    if b == 0:
        raise ValueError("Cannot divide by zero")
```

```
    return a / b
```

Congratulations! You've just created a module. Let's see how you can use this module in another Python script.

Importing Your Module

To use the functions defined in `mymath.py`, you need to import it into your main Python file. Create a new file named `main.py` and add the following code:

```python
# main.py

import mymath

def main():
    x = 10
    y = 5

    print(f"Add: {mymath.add(x, y)}")
    print(f"Subtract: {mymath.subtract(x, y)}")
    print(f"Multiply: {mymath.multiply(x, y)}")
```

```
    print(f"Divide: {mymath.divide(x, y)}")

if __name__ == "__main__":
    main()
```

Now, when you run `main.py`, it will output:

```
Add: 15
Subtract: 5
Multiply: 50
Divide: 2.0
```

This demonstrates how you can import and use the functions you've defined in `mymath` module. The `import mymath` statement fetches all the functions and variables defined in `mymath.py`, making them available in `main.py`.

Organizing Multiple Modules

In a real-world project, you may have multiple custom modules. To keep things organized, you can store your modules in a directory.

Consider the following structure:

```
project/
│
├── math_utils/
│   └── mymath.py
│
└── main.py
```

In this structure, you place `mymath.py` in a subfolder named `math_utils`.

To import `mymath` in this structure, you need to modify the import statement in `main.py` like so:

```python
from math_utils import mymath

def main():
    x = 10
    y = 5
```

```
    print(f"Add: {mymath.add(x, y)}")
    print(f"Subtract: {mymath.subtract(x, y)}")
    print(f"Multiply: {mymath.multiply(x, y)}")
    print(f"Divide: {mymath.divide(x, y)}")

if __name__ == "__main__":
    main()
```

This approach helps you maintain a clean and organized project structure, particularly useful in larger projects.

Conclusion

Creating your own modules is an essential skill in Python that vastly improves code manageability and reusability. As your projects grow, leveraging modules will become second nature, helping you to keep your code organized and maintainable. So go ahead, experiment with creating your custom modules, and take one step closer to becoming a proficient Python programmer.

Chapter 4: Object-Oriented Programming

Classes and Objects

In the journey of learning Python, a fundamental concept that you will encounter is object-oriented programming (OOP). A pivotal part of OOP is understanding classes and objects. These concepts form the backbone of many Python programs, offering a structured way to organize and approach code logically and efficiently.

What is a Class?

A class in Python can be thought of as a blueprint for creating objects. It defines a set of attributes and methods that the created objects—instances of the class—will possess. Classes help in encapsulating data and functions into one seamless unit.

Consider a class as a template; for example, let's say you want to model a car. The class `Car` would include attributes such as color, make, model, and year. It would also include methods, which are functions designed to work with these attributes, such as `start_engine()`, `stop_engine()`, and `accelerate()`.

Here is a basic example of a class in Python:

```python
class Car:
    def __init__(self, make, model, year):
        self.make = make
        self.model = model
        self.year = year

    def start_engine(self):
        print(f"The engine of the {self.year} {self.make} {self.model} starts.")

    def stop_engine(self):
        print(f"The engine of the {self.year} {self.make} {self.model} stops.")
```

In the above example, the `__init__` method is a special method that initializes an instance of the class. It is called a constructor and is automatically invoked when a new object is created.

What is an Object?

Objects are instances of classes. An object in Python is an entity that contains both data (attributes) and functionalities (methods). When you create an object from a class, you instantiate it, bringing the blueprint to life.

Let's create a couple of objects from the `Car` class to see this in action:

```python
my_car = Car("Toyota", "Camry", 2021)
your_car = Car("Honda", "Civic", 2020)

my_car.start_engine()
your_car.start_engine()
```

When we run the above code, we'll receive the following output:

```
The engine of the 2021 Toyota Camry starts.
The engine of the 2020 Honda Civic starts.
```

Here, `my_car` and `your_car` are two distinct objects that are instances of the `Car` class. Each object holds its own data, which is why `my_car` references a Toyota Camry and `your_car` references a Honda Civic.

Attributes and Methods

Attributes are variables that belong to an object, while methods are functions that belong to an object. As demonstrated, you can access the attributes using the dot notation (e.g., `my_car.make`) and invoke methods similarly.

One of the advantages of using classes and objects is code reusability. By defining a class, you can create multiple objects from the same blueprint without writing duplicate code. This allows for cleaner, more manageable, and modular code.

Encapsulation

Encapsulation is one of the four fundamental OOP concepts, along with inheritance, polymorphism, and abstraction. It is the mechanism of hiding a class's internal data and restricting direct access to some of the attributes. Instead, access to the data is provided through public methods. This ensures that the internal representation of an object is protected from unintended or harmful modifications.

You can achieve encapsulation in Python by prefixing an attribute name with an underscore (`_`) or double underscore (`__`). For instance:

```python
class Car:
    def __init__(self, make, model, year):
        self.__make = make  # private attribute
        self.__model = model  # private attribute
        self.__year = year  # private attribute

    def start_engine(self):
        print(f"The engine of the {self.__year} {self.__make} {self.__model} starts.")
```

In this example, attributes `__make`, `__model`, and `__year` are private and should not be accessed directly from outside the class. You would need to define public methods to retrieve or modify these attributes if necessary.

By understanding and employing classes and objects, you can enhance the organization and robustness of your code, making it easier to expand, maintain, and debug. Embarking on this chapter equips you with a powerful toolset essential for tackling complex programming challenges in a more manageable and scalable fashion.

Attributes and Methods

In the world of object-oriented programming (OOP), understanding attributes and methods is crucial for mastering the core concepts of the paradigm. Attributes and methods form the backbone of objects, encapsulating both data and behavior, respectively. To grasp these concepts, let's dive deeper into their definitions and practical applications within Python.

Attributes: The Properties of Objects

Attributes are variables that belong to an object or class. They store information relevant to the object and define its state. Consider attributes as the characteristics or properties that help describe an object. For instance, if we have a class `Car`, attributes might include `make`, `model`, `year`, and `color`.

Here's a simple example:

```python
class Car:
```

```
    def __init__(self, make, model, year, color):
        self.make = make
        self.model = model
        self.year = year
        self.color = color

# Creating an object of the Car class
my_car = Car("Toyota", "Corolla", 2020, "Red")

# Accessing attributes
print(my_car.make)   # Output: Toyota
print(my_car.model)  # Output: Corolla
print(my_car.year)   # Output: 2020
print(my_car.color)  # Output: Red
```

In this example, `__init__` is a special method called a constructor. It initializes an object's attributes when an instance of the class is created. The `self` parameter refers to the instance of the class and is used to access class attributes.

Methods: The Actions of Objects

Methods are functions defined inside a class that describe the behaviors of an object. They operate on the object's attributes and can perform operations on them. Think of methods as the actions that objects can perform. For example, a `Car` object might have methods like `start_engine`, `drive`, and `stop_engine`.

Here's how you can define and use methods in a class:

```python
class Car:
    def __init__(self, make, model, year, color):
        self.make = make
        self.model = model
        self.year = year
        self.color = color

    def start_engine(self):
        print(f"The {self.year} {self.make} {self.model} engine is now running.")

    def drive(self):
        print(f"The {self.color} {self.make} {self.model} is now driving.")

# Creating an object of the Car class
my_car = Car("Toyota", "Corolla", 2020, "Red")
```

```
# Calling methods
my_car.start_engine()  # Output: The 2020 Toyota Corolla engine is now running.
my_car.drive()  # Output: The Red Toyota Corolla is now driving.
```

Instance vs Class Attributes

Attributes can be classified as instance attributes or class attributes. Instance attributes are unique to each object, whereas class attributes are shared among all instances of the class.

Let's illustrate with an example:

```python
class Car:
    wheels = 4  # Class attribute

    def __init__(self, make, model, year, color):
        self.make = make  # Instance attribute
        self.model = model  # Instance attribute
        self.year = year  # Instance attribute
        self.color = color  # Instance attribute
```

```python
# Creating objects of the Car class
car1 = Car("Toyota", "Corolla", 2020, "Red")
car2 = Car("Honda", "Civic", 2019, "Blue")

# Accessing class attribute
print(Car.wheels)  # Output: 4

# Accessing instance attributes
print(car1.make)  # Output: Toyota
print(car2.model)  # Output: Civic

# Accessing class attribute through an instance
print(car1.wheels)  # Output: 4
print(car2.wheels)  # Output: 4
```

Methods vs Functions

It's important to distinguish between methods and functions. Methods are functions that belong to a class and operate on its instances, while functions are standalone blocks of code that perform a task independently of any class.

Encapsulation

Encapsulation is an OOP principle where the internal state of an object is hidden from the outside world and can only be accessed through methods. This provides data protection and abstraction, ensuring that objects control their own state.

```python
class Car:
    def __init__(self, make, model, year, color):
        self.make = make
        self.model = model
        self.__year = year  # Private attribute
        self.__color = color  # Private attribute

    def get_year(self):
        return self.__year

    def set_year(self, year):
        if year > 1885:  # Basic validation
            self.__year = year
        else:
            print("Invalid year")
```

```python
# Creating an object of the Car class
my_car = Car("Toyota", "Corolla", 2020, "Red")

# Accessing private attribute through a method
print(my_car.get_year())  # Output: 2020

# Trying to set an invalid year
my_car.set_year(1800)  # Output: Invalid year
```

In this example, the `__year` and `__color` attributes are private and can only be accessed through the public methods `get_year` and `set_year`.

By comprehending attributes and methods, you're well on your way to creating robust, flexible, and reusable code in Python. These foundational blocks will pave the path for more advanced OOP techniques and design patterns, enriching your programming prowess.

Inheritance

Imagine you're building a complex software application, one that needs multiple types of user accounts like "StandardUser," "AdminUser," and "GuestUser." You notice all these different accounts share common attributes, such as usernames and passwords, as well as similar behaviors like logging in and logging out. Wouldn't it be convenient if you could somehow define these common features in one place, rather than repeating them for each account type?

This is where Inheritance comes into play in Object-Oriented Programming (OOP). In Python, inheritance allows you to create a new class that is a modified version of an existing class. The new class, often referred to as the child or derived class, inherits attributes and behaviors (methods) from the existing class, which is called the parent or base class.

The Basics of Inheritance

Let's start with a simple example. Suppose we have a base class called `User`. This class includes essential attributes and methods common to all user types:

```python
class User:
    def __init__(self, username, password):
        self.username = username
        self.password = password
```

```python
    def login(self):
        print(f'{self.username} has logged in.')

    def logout(self):
        print(f'{self.username} has logged out.')
```

This `User` class can be extended by other classes. For instance, let's create an `AdminUser` class that inherits from `User`:

```python
class AdminUser(User):
    def __init__(self, username, password, permissions):
        super().__init__(username, password)  # Inherit username and password initialization
        self.permissions = permissions

    def show_permissions(self):
        print(f'Admin permissions: {self.permissions}')
```

In the `AdminUser` class, we use the `super()` function to call the `__init__` method of the base class `User`. This ensures `username` and `password` are initialized correctly. We also add an additional attribute, `permissions`, specific to `AdminUser`.

Overriding Methods

Sometimes, a child class may need to change the behavior of a method inherited from the parent class. This process is called method overriding.

For example, if we want to provide a custom login message for `AdminUser`, we can override the `login` method:

```python
class AdminUser(User):
    def __init__(self, username, password, permissions):
        super().__init__(username, password)
        self.permissions = permissions

    def login(self):
        print(f'{self.username} (Admin) has logged in.')
```

Now, when an instance of `AdminUser` calls the `login` method, the new message will be printed instead of the one defined in the `User` class.

Inheritance and Polymorphism

Inheritance is closely related to another key OOP concept: polymorphism. Polymorphism allows methods to be used interchangeably, even if they're defined in different classes. Consider this scenario:

```python
class GuestUser(User):
    def login(self):
        print(f'{self.username} (Guest) has logged in.')

users = [AdminUser('admin', '1234', 'all'), GuestUser('guest', 'guest')]
for user in users:
    user.login()
```

In the above code, despite the `login` method being overridden differently in `AdminUser` and `GuestUser`, we can still iterate through the `users` list and call `login()` on each user object without having to worry about their specific type. This is polymorphism at work.

Multiple Inheritance

Unlike some programming languages that support only single inheritance, Python allows multiple inheritance. This means a class can inherit from more than one base class.

For example:

```python
class Notifiable:
    def send_notification(self, message):
        print(f'Notification: {message}')

class AdminUser(User, Notifiable):
    def __init__(self, username, password, permissions):
        super().__init__(username, password)
        self.permissions = permissions

admin = AdminUser('admin', '1234', 'all')
admin.send_notification('System maintenance at midnight.')
```

In this case, `AdminUser` inherits from both `User` and `Notifiable`, gaining the ability to send notifications in addition to the user login functionalities.

Conclusion

Inheritance is a powerful feature in Python that promotes code reusability and efficiency. By extending existing classes, you can create new functionality with minimal code duplication. Understanding how to leverage inheritance effectively allows you to write more organized, scalable, and maintainable code. Whether you're a beginner or an experienced programmer, mastering inheritance will undoubtedly elevate your coding prowess.

Polymorphism

Polymorphism is one of the fundamental principles of object-oriented programming (OOP) that allows for flexibility and the integration of different data types and classes. In simple terms, polymorphism allows objects to be treated as instances of their parent class rather than their actual class. This means one interface can be used for a general class of actions, which can be refined for specific cases.

For example, consider a class hierarchy representing different types of animals. Each class might define a method called `speak`. For a `Dog` class, `speak` might involve barking, while for a `Cat` class, it might involve meowing. Polymorphism allows us to invoke `speak` on a collection of animals, each one of which may react differently despite invoking the same method.

Here's a Python example to illustrate this concept:

```python
class Animal:
    def speak(self):
        raise NotImplementedError("Subclass must implement abstract method")

class Dog(Animal):
    def speak(self):
        return "Woof!"

class Cat(Animal):
    def speak(self):
        return "Meow!"

def make_animal_speak(animal: Animal):
    print(animal.speak())

animals = [Dog(), Cat()]
```

```
for animal in animals:
    make_animal_speak(animal)
```

In this example, the `Animal` class defines a method called `speak`, which raises an error if it's not implemented by a subclass. Both the `Dog` and `Cat` classes implement this method. When the `make_animal_speak` function is called with different objects of `Animal` type, it generates outputs based on the actual class of the object, thanks to polymorphism.

Polymorphism is not limited to classes in a hierarchy. It can also be achieved through method overloading and operator overloading. While Python doesn't support traditional method overloading like some other languages, it allows operator overloading, which is another form of polymorphism.

Let's take a straightforward example with operator overloading:

```python
class Vector:
    def __init__(self, x, y):
        self.x = x
```

```
        self.y = y

    def __add__(self, other):
        return Vector(self.x + other.x, self.y + other.y)

    def __str__(self):
        return f"({self.x}, {self.y})"

vector1 = Vector(2, 3)
vector2 = Vector(1, 1)
vector3 = vector1 + vector2

print(vector3)  # Output: (3, 4)
```

In this instance, the `__add__` method of the `Vector` class allows vectors to be added together using the `+` operator. This technique provides the benefits of polymorphism by enabling the familiar `+` operator to work with a new data type, `Vector`.

Python also supports polymorphism through duck typing, another critical concept. Duck typing refers to Python's ability to use any object that provides the required methods and properties, rather than checking the object's type. It gets its name from the saying, "If it looks like a duck and quacks like a duck, it's probably a duck."

Here is a duck typing example:

```python
class Bird:
    def quack(self):
        return "Quack!"

class Human:
    def quack(self):
        return "I am quacking like a bird!"

def make_it_quack(thing):
    print(thing.quack())

quacky_things = [Bird(), Human()]

for thing in quacky_things:
    make_it_quack(thing)
```

In this script, both `Bird` and `Human` classes have a `quack` method. The function `make_it_quack` does not care about the type of object it is acting on; it only cares that the object provides a `quack` method. This flexibility is what makes polymorphism a powerful tool in Python programming, promoting code reusability and scalability.

To conclude, grasping polymorphism opens the door to writing more robust and adaptable code. By utilizing unified interfaces, method overriding, and Python's dynamic nature, polymorphism paves the way for building software that is not just functional but also elegant.

Encapsulation

Encapsulation, one of the fundamental principles of object-oriented programming (OOP), is often described as a protective barrier that prevents the code and data within a class from being freely accessed and modified by outside interference. It's essentially about bundling the data (variables) and the code (methods) that operate on the data into a single unit known as a class, and controlling the access to that bundle.

In Python, encapsulation is achieved using private and protected members. Private members are those that cannot be accessed outside the class, while protected members are intended to be accessible only within the class and its subclasses. Python uses name mangling to make a member private by prefixing the member name with double underscores (`__`).

Here is a basic example to illustrate encapsulation:

```python
class Car:
    def __init__(self, make, model, year):
        self.make = make
        self._model = model  # Protected attribute
        self.__year = year   # Private attribute

    def get_year(self):
        return self.__year

    def set_year(self, year):
        if year > 1885:  # Setting a condition to ensure a valid year
            self.__year = year

    def describe_car(self):
            return f"This car is a {self.make} {self._model} from {self.__year}."

# Creating a new Car object
my_car = Car('Toyota', 'Corolla', 2020)
```

```python
# Accessing the public attribute
print(my_car.make)  # Output: Toyota

# Accessing the protected attribute (not recommended)
print(my_car._model)  # Output: Corolla

# Attempting to access the private attribute directly will result in an error
# print(my_car.__year)  # AttributeError: 'Car' object has no attribute '__year'

# Accessing the private attribute using getter method
print(my_car.get_year())  # Output: 2020

# Setting a new year using the setter method
my_car.set_year(2021)
print(my_car.get_year())  # Output: 2021

# Print description of the car
print(my_car.describe_car())  # Output: This car is a Toyota Corolla from 2021.
```

In this example, `make` is a public attribute, `_model` is a protected attribute, and `__year` is a private attribute. Accessing a private attribute directly, like `my_car.__year`, would raise an `AttributeError`. Instead, we use getter and setter methods (`get_year` and `set_year`) to work with the private attribute, ensuring controlled access and modification.

The underscore convention and double underscore prefix in Python are not absolute and can be bypassed, but they serve as a strong indication to other developers about how these variables should be accessed. Following these conventions ensures that the internal state of an object is protected and maintained in a controlled manner, reducing the risk of unintended side effects or bugs.

Encapsulation promotes data hiding and abstraction, leading to more secure and maintainable code. It ensures that objects manage their own state and behavior in a consistent manner and present a clean interface to the outside world. By carefully designing classes with proper encapsulation, developers can create robust, reliable applications where internal implementation details are kept safely hidden from the rest of the system.

Magic Methods

When you delve deeper into Python, you will inevitably encounter magic methods, sometimes referred to as dunder (double underscore) methods. These special methods allow you to define the behavior of your objects for fundamental operations like arithmetic, comparison, and even being converted to strings. Magic methods are crucial for making your classes behave more like built-in Python types.

At the heart of magic methods is the philosophy of Python: to make your objects as intuitive and functional as possible. One of the most commonly used magic methods is `__init__`, which initializes an object's attributes. However, there are many more, each unlocking a different aspect of functionality.

Let's start with the `__str__` and `__repr__` methods, which control how an object is represented as a string. The `__str__` method is aimed at creating a readable and user-friendly string representation of an object, typically for logging or displaying to end-users.

```python
class Fruit:
    def __init__(self, name, color):
        self.name = name
        self.color = color
```

```
    def __str__(self):
        return f"A {self.color} {self.name}"
```

With this `Fruit` class, the `__str__` method ensures that printing an instance of `Fruit` will yield a friendly message:

```python
apple = Fruit("apple", "red")
print(apple)  # Output: A red apple
```

On the other hand, the `__repr__` method is meant to provide an unambiguous string representation of an object, often one that could be used to recreate the object. As a best practice, you should implement `__repr__` for your classes:

```python
class Fruit:
    def __init__(self, name, color):
        self.name = name
        self.color = color

    def __repr__(self):
```

```
        return f"Fruit(name={self.name}, color={self.color})"
```

Now, if you use the `repr` function or inspect an object directly, you'll get a more informative output:

```python
banana = Fruit("banana", "yellow")
print(repr(banana))  # Output: Fruit(name=banana, color=yellow)
```

Next up are arithmetic magic methods like `__add__`, `__sub__`, and `__mul__`, which allow your objects to respond to operators such as `+`, `-`, and `*`. For instance, let's imagine a simple `Vector` class that supports vector addition:

```python
class Vector:
    def __init__(self, x, y):
        self.x = x
        self.y = y

    def __add__(self, other):
        return Vector(self.x + other.x, self.y + other.y)
```

```python
    def __repr__(self):
        return f"Vector(x={self.x}, y={self.y})"
```

With this setup, you can now add two `Vector` instances seamlessly:

```python
v1 = Vector(2, 3)
v2 = Vector(5, 7)
print(v1 + v2)  # Output: Vector(x=7, y=10)
```

Python also allows you to craft custom behavior with comparison operators through methods like `__eq__`, `__lt__`, and `__gt__`. Let's illustrate this by implementing the `__eq__` method to make two `Point` objects comparable based on their coordinates:

```python
class Point:
    def __init__(self, x, y):
        self.x = x
        self.y = y
```

```
    def __eq__(self, other):
        return self.x == other.x and self.y == other.y

    def __repr__(self):
        return f"Point(x={self.x}, y={self.y})"
```

Now, you can check if two points are equal:

```python
p1 = Point(1, 2)
p2 = Point(1, 2)
p3 = Point(3, 4)
print(p1 == p2)  # Output: True
print(p1 == p3)  # Output: False
```

By understanding and utilizing magic methods, you grant your objects all the expressive and functional power of native Python types. They allow your classes to integrate smoothly with Python's syntax and operations, providing a richer and more intuitive interface for users of your code. As you continue to explore these special methods, you'll unlock new layers of Python's object-oriented capabilities, making your code both elegant and, importantly, Pythonic.

Using OOP in Real Projects

When it comes to applying Object-Oriented Programming (OOP) in real projects, the benefits truly shine. Let's explore how you can harness the power of OOP to enhance your Python projects, making them more modular, reusable, and easier to maintain.

Imagine you're building a simple e-commerce application. One of the core elements of such a system is the concept of a `Product`. In a procedural programming approach, you might use separate functions to handle different aspects of a product's lifecycle. However, this can quickly become cumbersome as your codebase grows. In contrast, OOP allows you to encapsulate product-related data and behaviors into a single `Product` class.

```python
class Product:
    def __init__(self, name, price, quantity):
        self.name = name
        self.price = price
        self.quantity = quantity

    def update_price(self, new_price):
        self.price = new_price
```

```python
    def update_quantity(self, new_quantity):
        self.quantity = new_quantity

    def get_total_value(self):
        return self.price * self.quantity

# Creating instances of the Product class
iphone = Product('iPhone', 999, 5)
macbook = Product('MacBook', 1299, 3)

# Updating product data
iphone.update_price(949)
macbook.update_quantity(4)

# Calculating total value
print(iphone.get_total_value())  # Output: 4745
print(macbook.get_total_value())  # Output: 5196
```

In this example, the `Product` class encapsulates all data and methods related to a product. Each instance of the class represents a unique product with its own attributes and behaviors. This modular approach makes the code more organized and easier to manage.

But OOP doesn't stop at encapsulation. Another powerful feature is inheritance. Let's say you want to add different types of products, such as perishable goods that have an expiration date. Instead of rewriting the entire `Product` class, you can create a subclass that inherits from it and extends its functionality.

```python
class PerishableProduct(Product):
    def __init__(self, name, price, quantity, expiration_date):
        super().__init__(name, price, quantity)
        self.expiration_date = expiration_date

    def is_expired(self, current_date):
        return current_date > self.expiration_date

# Creating an instance of PerishableProduct
milk = PerishableProduct('Milk', 3, 10, '2023-12-01')

# Checking if the product is expired
print(milk.is_expired('2023-10-01'))  # Output: False
```

This example demonstrates how inheritance allows you to build upon existing code, promoting code reuse and reducing redundancy. The `PerishableProduct` class inherits the attributes and methods of the `Product` class and adds its own unique behavior.

Another key concept in OOP is polymorphism, which allows objects of different classes to be treated as objects of a common superclass. This can be especially useful when you need to write generic code that works with various types of objects. For instance, if you have a list of different product types and you want to calculate their total value, polymorphism lets you do this seamlessly.

```python
def calculate_total_inventory_value(products):
    total_value = 0
    for product in products:
        total_value += product.get_total_value()
    return total_value

# List of products
products = [iphone, macbook, milk]
print(calculate_total_inventory_value(products))  # Output: 9941
```

Here, the `calculate_total_inventory_value` function can work with any product object that has a `get_total_value` method, regardless of its specific subclass. This flexibility simplifies code maintenance and makes it easier to extend functionality in the future.

Using OOP in real projects isn't just about following a programming paradigm; it's about leveraging a set of tools and concepts that can make your code more robust, scalable, and easier to understand. By encapsulating data and behaviors, promoting code reuse through inheritance, and enabling flexible and generic programming with polymorphism, OOP empowers you to tackle complex programming challenges with confidence.

Chapter 5: Exception Handling and Debugging

Understanding Exceptions

Imagine you're cooking a complicated recipe. You're following every step meticulously, but suddenly, you notice you're out of a crucial ingredient. What do you do? You probably don't discard the entire dish. Instead, you either find a substitute or change your cooking method slightly to adapt to the situation. In programming, exceptions are the missing ingredients, the unexpected errors that can occur, and exception handling is how we deal with them without abandoning our whole program.

To understand exceptions in Python, think of them as problems that disrupt the normal flow of your program. When such a disruption occurs, Python creates an exception object. If this object isn't dealt with properly, it leads to the crashing of your program. Handling exceptions is like having a Plan B, ensuring that your program can manage the problem and, if possible, continue to run smoothly.

Types of Exceptions

Python has many built-in exceptions, each corresponding to a different error type. Here are some of the most common ones:

- **`ZeroDivisionError`**: This exception occurs when you try to divide a number by zero.
- **`TypeError`**: This happens when an operation or function is applied to an object of an inappropriate type.
- **`ValueError`**: This arises when a function receives an argument of the correct type but inappropriate value.
- **`FileNotFoundError`**: As the name suggests, this exception is raised when trying to open a file that doesn't exist.

Why Exceptions Happen

Many things can go wrong when you run a program, leading to exceptions. Here are some typical scenarios:

1. **User Input Errors**: Users often provide input outside of what your program expects. For instance, if your program asks for a number and the user types in a string.
2. **File Operations**: Problems like trying to read a file that doesn't exist or doesn't have read permissions can cause exceptions.
3. **Resource Limitations**: Your program may attempt to use resources like memory or network bandwidth more than what's available.

Raising Exceptions

At times, you might want to trigger an exception deliberately using the `raise` statement. This practice is used to alert others who are using your code that something has gone wrong or doesn't make sense.

```python
def check_age(age):
    if age < 0:
        raise ValueError("Age cannot be negative")
    return "Valid age"
```

In the example above, if the `age` is less than zero, a `ValueError` is raised to alert that the input is not acceptable.

The `try` and `except` Block

The core of exception handling in Python is the `try` and `except` block structure. Here's how it works:

1. **`try` Block**: This block contains the code that might raise an exception.

2. **`except` Block**: This block catches and handles the exception.

```python
try:
    result = 10 / 0
except ZeroDivisionError:
    print("You cannot divide by zero!")
```

In this example, the code in the `try` block will raise a `ZeroDivisionError`, and the `except` block will catch it and print a user-friendly message instead of crashing the program.

Handling Multiple Exceptions

Sometimes, you might want to handle different exceptions differently. Python provides a way to catch multiple exceptions by specifying multiple `except` blocks.

```python
try:
    value = int(input("Enter a number: "))
    result = 10 / value
except ValueError:
```

    print("That's not a number!")
except ZeroDivisionError:
    print("You cannot divide by zero!")
```

**The `else` and `finally` Clauses**

You can also add `else` and `finally` clauses to a `try` block to make your exception handling more robust:

- **`else` Block**: Executes if the `try` block does not raise an exception.
- **`finally` Block**: Executes regardless of whether an exception occurred.

```python
try:
    with open("example.txt", "r") as file:
        data = file.read()
except FileNotFoundError:
    print("The file does not exist.")
else:
    print("File read successfully.")
finally:

```
    print("Execution complete.")
```

In this code, if the file is read successfully, the message "File read successfully" is printed, and the `finally` block runs no matter what, indicating that the program finished its execution path.

Understanding exceptions and how to handle them is crucial for writing robust and resilient programs. In essence, it transforms potential runtime errors from being catastrophic to being manageable blips in your code's execution flow. This doesn't just make your programs more reliable; it also makes them more user-friendly and professional.

Try and Except Blocks

In any programming language, errors are inevitable. When they happen, they can crash our programs and leave behind confusing error messages. To handle these errors gracefully, Python provides a powerful feature called exception handling. One of the primary constructs used for this in Python is the try and except block.

Why Use try and except?

Imagine you've written a program to read a file. The file exists on your machine, so everything works perfectly during development. But what if a user tries to run your program and the file isn't there? Normally, Python would throw an IOError, crashing your program. With the try and except mechanism, you can catch such errors and handle them more elegantly.

Basic Syntax

The basic structure of a try and except block looks like this:

```python
try:
    # Code that might raise an exception
    risky_code()
except SomeException as e:
    # Code that runs if an exception occurs
    handle_exception(e)
```

Here, `risky_code()` is the part of your code that might raise an exception. `SomeException` refers to the specific type of exception you're expecting. When an exception occurs, instead of halting execution, Python jumps to the `except` block and runs the code in that section.

Handling Multiple Exceptions

You might anticipate different types of exceptions arising from a block of code. Python allows you to handle multiple exceptions using multiple except clauses:

```python
try:
    # Code that might raise multiple exceptions
    another_risky_code()
except IOError as e:
    # Handle file-related errors
    handle_io_error(e)
except ValueError as e:
    # Handle value errors
    handle_value_error(e)
```

In this example, two different types of exceptions are caught: IOError and ValueError. Each has its own except block, enabling tailored responses to different error conditions.

Catching Any Exception

Sometimes, you might not know exactly what type of exception could be raised, or you might want a catch-all handler for unexpected issues. You can catch any exception by omitting the specific exception type:

```python
try:
    generic_risky_code()
except Exception as e:
    # Handle any exception
    handle_any_exception(e)
```

While this is convenient, use it sparingly. Catching all exceptions can make debugging harder because it can mask specific errors.

The else and finally Blocks

Python's exception handling blocks can also include `else` and `finally` clauses for additional control:

- **else**: The code in the else block runs if no exceptions were raised in the try block.

- **finally**: The code in the finally block always runs, no matter what. It's typically used for cleanup actions like closing files or releasing resources.

Example:

```python
try:
    # Code that might raise an exception
    yet_another_risky_code()
except SomeException as e:
    # Handle the exception
    handle_specific_exception(e)
else:
    # Code to run if no exception occurs
    no_exception_occurred()
finally:
    # Code to run no matter what
    cleanup()
```

Real-World Example

Consider a case where you're building a user-friendly calculator. You might want to catch errors for invalid inputs:

```python
def divide(x, y):
    try:
        result = x / y
    except ZeroDivisionError as e:
        print("Error: Cannot divide by zero!")
    except TypeError as e:
        print("Error: Invalid input type!")
    else:
        print("The result is:", result)
    finally:
        print("Execution completed.")

divide(10, 0)
divide(10, 'a')
divide(10, 2)
```

Output:

```
```

Error: Cannot divide by zero!
Execution completed.
Error: Invalid input type!
Execution completed.
The result is: 5.0
Execution completed.
```

In this example, the function handles different types of errors gracefully and ensures a message is always printed when execution is completed.

Understanding and using try and except blocks effectively can greatly enhance the robustness of your Python programs by making them more resilient to unexpected issues. This makes your applications not only more user-friendly but also easier to debug and maintain.

## Finally and Else Clauses

While working with exception handling in Python, the `try` and `except` blocks are fundamental. However, there's more depth to exception handling than just catching and handling exceptions. Two important parts of the `try` statement that are often overlooked are the `finally` and `else` clauses. These can significantly contribute to the robustness and clarity of your code.
```

The Finally Clause

The `finally` clause is designed for cleaning up actions that must be executed under all circumstances. Code within a `finally` block will always run, regardless of whether an exception was raised or not. This is particularly useful for releasing external resources like file handles or network connections, which should be cleaned up properly to avoid resource leaks.

Here is a basic example to illustrate the use of the `finally` clause:

```python
try:
    file = open('myfile.txt', 'r')
    content = file.read()
except FileNotFoundError:
    print("File not found.")
finally:
    if 'file' in locals():
        file.close()
        print("File has been closed.")
```

In this example, the `finally` block ensures that the file is closed whether or not an exception occurred. The `if 'file' in locals():` check might be necessary to ensure that the file object exists in the local namespace before attempting to close it, which can prevent a potential `NameError`.

The Else Clause

The `else` clause offers a simpler way to handle code that should run only if the `try` block did not raise an exception. This can be particularly useful to keep your code clean and separate the error handling from the "happy path" logic.

Here's a straightforward use case with the `else` clause:

```python
try:
    result = 10 / 2
except ZeroDivisionError:
    print("You can't divide by zero!")
else:
    print(f"The result is {result}")
finally:
    print("Execution has completed.")
```

In this example, the message `The result is 5.0` gets printed if there's no exception, otherwise the specific `ZeroDivisionError` message will be displayed. The `finally` block will execute regardless, displaying "Execution has completed."

Combining Finally and Else

While the combination of `else` and `finally` might be less common, it can be particularly powerful in certain situations.

Consider the following case:

```python
try:
    data = {"key": "value"}
    value = data["key"]
except KeyError:
    print("The key does not exist.")
else:
    print(f"Retrieved value: {value}")
finally:
    print("Cleaning up resources, if any.")
```

Here, the `else` clause is used to print the value only if there was no exception, and `finally` is used to print a message (and ideally perform any cleanup actions) irrespective of whether an exception occurred.

Practical Example: Network Connections
In a more complex scenario, such as managing network connections, both `else` and `finally` can be indispensable.

```python
import requests

try:
    response = requests.get('https://api.example.com/data')
    response.raise_for_status()  # This will raise an HTTPError if the HTTP request returned an unsuccessful status code
except requests.RequestException as e:
    print(f"An error occurred: {e}")
else:
    print("Request was successful.")
    data = response.json()
    print(data)
finally:
    print("Cleaning up the network resources.")
    # Here, you might close open sessions or handle other cleanup
```

actions.
```

In this snippet, the `else` block only runs if the network request is successful, ensuring that the data extraction and printing only occur when there are no exceptions. Meanwhile, the `finally` block is responsible for cleaning up, a placeholder for any necessary network resource cleanup.

### Conclusion

Incorporating `finally` and `else` clauses in your exception handling strategy can improve the robustness and readability of your Python code. Understanding these constructs not only helps in managing resources better but also makes your code easier to follow and maintain. The `finally` clause ensures that certain actions are always completed while the `else` clause clarifies logic that should only run in the absence of exceptions. Both are essential tools in a Python developer's toolkit, enabling more reliable and maintainable code.

# Raising Exceptions

Raising exceptions is a fundamental aspect of robust software development in Python. It allows you to handle error conditions gracefully and maintain the stability and reliability of your application. In this section, we'll explore how to raise exceptions effectively,
```

ensuring your code is not only functional but also resilient.

Why Raise Exceptions?

Exceptions provide a mechanism for flagging error conditions and unexpected behavior in your code. By raising exceptions, you clarify where and why an issue has occurred, providing a clear signal that something has gone awry. This can help you and other developers quickly diagnose problems and implement fixes.

The Basics of Raising Exceptions

In Python, the `raise` statement is used to raise an exception. The syntax is straightforward:

```python
raise ExceptionType("Error message")
```

Here, `ExceptionType` is the type of exception you want to raise, and `"Error message"` is an optional string providing additional information about the error.

For example, you might raise a `ValueError` if a function receives an argument that's outside the acceptable range:

```python
def divide(a, b):
    if b == 0:
        raise ValueError("The divisor 'b' cannot be zero.")
    return a / b
```

In this snippet, if the divisor `b` is zero, the `ValueError` is raised with a descriptive error message.

Custom Exceptions

Sometimes, the built-in exceptions aren't specific enough for your needs. In such cases, you can define your own exception classes by subclassing Python's built-in `Exception` class:

```python
class CustomError(Exception):
    pass
```

Custom exceptions can carry additional information beyond a simple error message. For instance, you might want to include metadata about the error:

```python
class CustomError(Exception):
    def __init__(self, message, error_code):
        super().__init__(message)
        self.error_code = error_code

try:
    raise CustomError("Something went wrong.", 404)
except CustomError as e:
    print(f"Error: {e}, Code: {e.error_code}")
```

By including an `error_code` in the `CustomError` class, you can capture and respond to specific error conditions more effectively.

When to Raise Exceptions

Knowing when to raise exceptions is crucial. Here are some guidelines:

1. **Invalid Arguments**: Raise exceptions when a function receives

arguments that are inappropriate or out of expected bounds.

2. **Unrecoverable States**: If the code reaches a state that cannot be resolved or corrected within the current context, an exception should signal that immediate attention is needed.

3. **Contract Violations**: When dealing with APIs or libraries, violations of expected contracts or interfaces should result in exceptions to notify developers of incorrect usage.

Propagating Exceptions

In many cases, you might not handle an exception where it's raised. Instead, you propagate the exception up the call stack, allowing higher-level functions or modules to manage it:

```python
def low_level_function():
    raise ValueError("A low-level error occurred.")

def high_level_function():
    try:
        low_level_function()
    except ValueError as e:
```

```
    print(f"Handled in high_level_function: {e}")

high_level_function()
```

Here, `high_level_function` catches the `ValueError` raised by `low_level_function` and handles it appropriately.

Conclusion

Raising exceptions is a powerful tool in Python, enabling you to manage errors and maintain control over your software's execution flow. By raising built-in or custom exceptions, you provide clear and actionable error messages, facilitating easier debugging and more robust applications. Remember to raise exceptions judiciously—use them to signal critical issues that cannot be ignored, ensuring your code remains clean and maintainable.

Custom Exceptions

In the world of programming, errors are inevitable. Whether they stem from incorrect user input, unexpected values, or logic mistakes, handling these errors gracefully is essential for creating robust, user-friendly applications. Standard exceptions provided by Python, such as `ValueError`, `TypeError`, and `IndexError`, cover many common scenarios. However, as you delve deeper into specialized code, you might encounter situations where standard exceptions fall short of conveying the specific nature of an error. In such cases, creating custom exceptions can offer more precise control and clarity.

Why Use Custom Exceptions?

Custom exceptions allow you to pinpoint the exact nature of an error, making your code more readable and maintainable. For instance, imagine you're developing an application to manage a library database. While standard exceptions can handle some errors, they cannot distinguish between a missing book, an overdue return, or unauthorized access. Custom exceptions allow you to target these specific scenarios more accurately.

Defining a Custom Exception

Creating a custom exception in Python involves subclassing the base `Exception` class or one of its subclasses. Here's a basic structure on how to define a custom exception:

```python
class LibraryError(Exception):
    """Base class for other exceptions in this module."""
```

```python
    pass


class BookNotFoundError(LibraryError):
    """Raised when a requested book does not exist in the library."""
    def __init__(self, book_title, message="Book not found in the library."):
        self.book_title = book_title
        self.message = message
        super().__init__(self.message)

    def __str__(self):
        return f'{self.book_title} -> {self.message}'


class OverdueBookError(LibraryError):
    """Raised when a book is overdue."""
    def __init__(self, book_title, days_overdue, message="Book is overdue."):
        self.book_title = book_title
        self.days_overdue = days_overdue
        self.message = message
        super().__init__(self.message)

    def __str__(self):
        return f'{self.book_title} is overdue by {self.days_overdue} days.
```

{self.message}'
```

Here, `LibraryError` serves as a base class for all library-related exceptions, ensuring a common hierarchy. `BookNotFoundError` and `OverdueBookError` are more specific exceptions that inherit from `LibraryError`. Note how we've used the `__init__` and `__str__` methods to initialize and return a meaningful error message.

**Raising Custom Exceptions**

Once you have defined your custom exceptions, raising them is straightforward. Use the `raise` keyword, just as you would with standard exceptions:

```python
def find_book(database, book_title):
    if book_title not in database:
        raise BookNotFoundError(book_title)
    return database[book_title]

def return_book(database, book_title, return_date, due_date):
    if return_date > due_date:
        days_overdue = (return_date - due_date).days

```
    raise OverdueBookError(book_title, days_overdue)
   # logic to return the book
```

In these functions, `find_book` raises a `BookNotFoundError` if the book is not in the database, and `return_book` raises an `OverdueBookError` if the book is returned late.

Handling Custom Exceptions

Handling custom exceptions involves the familiar `try`, `except`, and optionally `finally` constructs:

```python
try:
    book = find_book(library_db, "The Great Gatsby")
    return_book(library_db, "The Great Gatsby", datetime.date(2023, 5, 21), datetime.date(2023, 5, 14))
except BookNotFoundError as e:
    print(e)
except OverdueBookError as e:
    print(e)
```

This approach allows you to respond to specific issues with tailored messages or actions. For instance, the library system could automatically send a different notification to the user for a missing book versus an overdue book.

Best Practices for Custom Exceptions

1. **Clarity:** Ensure that custom exceptions are as clear and descriptive as possible. The name of the exception and its attributes should convey useful information.
2. **Documentation:** Document your custom exceptions well. Explain what conditions lead to each exception and its attributes.
3. **Hierarchy:** Organize custom exceptions into a clear hierarchy. Pair all domain-specific exceptions under a common base class to simplify exception handling.
4. **Use Sparingly:** Don't overuse custom exceptions. If a standard exception will suffice, there's no need to create a new one.

Custom exceptions provide a powerful way to handle errors more gracefully and precisely. They not only help in debugging but also make your code cleaner and more understandable. By following best practices, you can leverage custom exceptions to create more robust and maintainable Python applications.

Debugging Techniques

When you're diving deep into the world of Python programming, encountering bugs is an inevitable part of the journey. These issues can range from simple syntax errors to more complex runtime anomalies. In this subchapter, we'll explore several debugging techniques to help you identify and fix these problems effectively.

1. Print Statements

The simplest and often most effective debugging tool is adding print statements to your code. By printing variables and program states at various points, you can trace the flow of execution and understand where things might be going wrong.

For instance, assume you are working on a function that calculates the factorial of a number:
```python
def factorial(n):
    result = 1
    for i in range(1, n+1):
        result *= i
    return result
```

If the result is not what you expect, you can insert print statements:

```python
def factorial(n):
    result = 1
    for i in range(1, n+1):
        result *= i
        print(f"i: {i}, result: {result}")
    return result
```

This way, you can see the intermediate values of `i` and `result` as the function runs.

2. Using Debuggers

Python comes equipped with a powerful debugging tool, the Python Debugger (pdb). By inserting `import pdb; pdb.set_trace()` in your code, you can pause execution and inspect variables, step through code line by line, and continue execution.

Consider the previous factorial function:

```python
import pdb

def factorial(n):
```

```
    pdb.set_trace()
    result = 1
    for i in range(1, n+1):
        result *= i
    return result
```

Run the script, and once it hits the `pdb.set_trace()` line, you'll enter an interactive debugging session where you can use commands like `n` (next) to step through code, `p <variable>` to print a variable's value, and `c` (continue) to resume execution.

3. Logging

When a program grows in complexity, print statements might become cluttered and hard to manage. Instead, consider using the `logging` module. It offers a flexible framework for emitting log messages from your code, which can be output to various destinations, including the console or a file.

Example:
```python
import logging

logging.basicConfig(level=logging.DEBUG, format='%(asctime)s -
```

```
                    %(levelname)s - %(message)s')

def factorial(n):
    result = 1
    for i in range(1, n+1):
        result *= i
        logging.debug(f"i: {i}, result: {result}")
    return result
```

Configuring the logging level to `DEBUG` ensures that all debug messages will be output. You can easily change the configuration to suppress debugging information in a production environment.

4. Exception Handling

Using try-except blocks allows you to handle potential errors gracefully. More importantly, during debugging, you can capture and log detailed information about exceptions:

```python
def divide(a, b):
    try:
        result = a / b
    except ZeroDivisionError as e:
        logging.error(f"ZeroDivisionError: {e}")
```

        result = None
    return result
```

In this example, if a division by zero occurs, the error is caught, an error message is logged, and the function returns `None`.

### 5. Code Reviews and Pair Programming

Sometimes, a fresh set of eyes can catch issues you might have overlooked. Code reviews and pair programming involve other developers reviewing your code or working alongside you. This collaborative approach can be invaluable for identifying bugs and improving code quality.

### 6. Automated Testing

Incorporating automated tests into your development process can preemptively catch bugs. Use frameworks like `unittest` or `pytest` to write test cases for your code. These tests can run after every change to ensure that new bugs are not introduced:

```python
import unittest

def add(x, y):

```
    return x + y

class TestMathFunctions(unittest.TestCase):
    def test_add(self):
        self.assertEqual(add(2, 3), 5)
        self.assertEqual(add(-1, 1), 0)
        self.assertEqual(add(0, 0), 0)

if __name__ == '__main__':
    unittest.main()
```

Make it a habit to write tests for new features and bug fixes to keep your codebase robust.

7. Integrated Development Environments (IDEs)

IDEs like PyCharm, Visual Studio Code, and others come with built-in debugging tools. These IDEs offer advanced features such as breakpoints, watch expressions, and call stack navigation that simplify the debugging process.

By mastering these debugging techniques, you'll become more adept at identifying and resolving issues in your code. Debugging is as much an art as it is a science, and with practice, you'll learn to track down even the most elusive bugs with confidence.

Using pdb for Debugging

When it comes to debugging Python code, the `pdb` module is an invaluable tool that can greatly enhance your productivity and understanding of how your code operates. In this subchapter, we will explore the essentials of using `pdb` to effectively debug your Python programs.

Getting Started with `pdb`

The Python Debugger, commonly referred to as `pdb`, is a built-in module that allows you to set breakpoints, step through code, inspect variables, and evaluate expressions at runtime. To start using `pdb`, you can invoke it directly in your script by importing the module and setting breakpoints.

Here is a simple example to demonstrate its basic functionality:

```python
import pdb

def add_numbers(a, b):
    result = a + b
```

```
    pdb.set_trace()  # This sets a breakpoint
    return result

print(add_numbers(3, 5))
```

In this code snippet, `pdb.set_trace()` pauses the execution of the program and opens an interactive debugging session when the function `add_numbers` is called.

Basic Commands

Once you are in the interactive `pdb` shell, you'll find a range of commands at your disposal. Here are some of the most commonly used ones:

- `n` or `next`: Executes the next line of code but does not step into functions.
- `s` or `step`: Steps into the function and stops at the first line within it.
- `c` or `continue`: Continues execution until the next breakpoint.
- `q` or `quit`: Quits the debugging session.

For example, if you were to run the previous script and the execution pauses at `pdb.set_trace()`, you can type `n` to move to the next line, which will decrement the line pointer and execute the line `result = a + b`.

Inspecting Variables

Inspecting variable values is essential to understand the state of your program at any point in time. Inside the `pdb` shell, you can inspect variables simply by typing their names:

```python
> .../script.py(5)add_numbers()
-> return result
(Pdb) result
8
(Pdb) a
3
(Pdb) b
5
```

This allows you to see the current values of `result`, `a`, and `b`, providing you with insights into what is happening inside your code.

Setting Breakpoints

You can set additional breakpoints in your code by using the `break` command in the `pdb` shell. Breakpoints can be set in specific lines or functions:

```python
(Pdb) break 3
Breakpoint 1 at .../script.py:3
(Pdb) break add_numbers
Breakpoint 2 at .../script.py:1
```

These breakpoints will pause the execution when these lines or functions are encountered, allowing for more control over the debugging process.

Advanced Features

Once you are comfortable with the basics, `pdb` offers more advanced features like conditional breakpoints and post-mortem debugging.

- **Conditional Breakpoints**: These can be set to trigger only when certain conditions are met.

```python
(Pdb) break 5, result > 10
```

- **Post-Mortem Debugging**: This lets you start debugging after an exception has occurred, providing an opportunity to inspect the state of the program at the point of failure.

```python
import pdb
import sys

try:
    raise ValueError("An example exception")
except ValueError as e:
    _, _, tb = sys.exc_info()
    pdb.post_mortem(tb)
```

Using these advanced techniques enables more precise and efficient debugging, especially when dealing with complex code bases.

Conclusion

Mastering `pdb` takes practice, but the time invested in learning this powerful tool will pay off in the long run. Debugging can be a daunting task, particularly in larger programs, but `pdb` provides the necessary means to dissect your code methodically. By employing the various commands and functionality discussed in this subchapter, you will be well on your way to becoming proficient in debugging Python code.

Chapter 6: Working with Files

Reading Files

Reading files in Python is a fundamental skill every programmer should master. Whether it's reading configuration files, text logs, or data files for processing, the simplicity and power Python offers can make your work efficient and less error-prone.

Opening a File

The first step in reading a file is to open it. Python provides the built-in `open()` function for this purpose. This function returns a file object, which has methods and attributes to help you read files. Here's the basic syntax:

```python
file_object = open("filename", "mode")
```

The `filename` is a string that holds the name of the file, and the `mode` determines how the file will be opened. For reading, you'll primarily use the `'r'` mode, which stands for "read."

Reading the Entire File

One common way to read the contents of a file is to use the `read()` method, which reads the entire file into a single string. Here's a simple example:

```python
with open("example.txt", "r") as file:
    content = file.read()
    print(content)
```

In this example, the `with` statement automatically manages file closing, so there's no need to explicitly call `file.close()`. The `content` variable will hold the entire file's data as a string.

Reading Line-by-Line

Sometimes, you need to process a file line-by-line. You can achieve this using the `readline()` or `readlines()` methods. The `readline()` method reads one complete line from a file, while `readlines()` reads all lines into a list.

Here's an example using `readline()`:

```python
with open("example.txt", "r") as file:
    line = file.readline()
    while line:
        print(line.strip())  # Strip is used to remove the newline character
        line = file.readline()
```

And here's an example using `readlines()`:

```python
with open("example.txt", "r") as file:
    lines = file.readlines()
    for line in lines:
        print(line.strip())
```

Efficient File Reading

For sizeable files, reading the entire file at once might not be efficient. In such cases, you can read the file in chunks or use a loop for incremental reading.

Here's an example of reading a file in chunks:

```python
with open("largefile.txt", "r") as file:
    chunk_size = 1024  # Read in 1KB chunks
    chunk = file.read(chunk_size)
    while chunk:
        print(chunk, end='')
        chunk = file.read(chunk_size)
```

Working with File Paths

In many projects, you won't be working with files in the same directory as your script. Python's `os.path` module can help you navigate and manipulate file paths.

Here's an example:

```python
import os

file_path = os.path.join("folder", "subfolder", "example.txt")
with open(file_path, "r") as file:
    print(file.read())
```

```

### Error Handling

Reading files often involves error handling. What if the file doesn't exist or if the program doesn't have permission to read the file? Python excels in exception handling using `try` and `except` blocks.

Here's an example:

```python
try:
    with open("example.txt", "r") as file:
        print(file.read())
except FileNotFoundError:
    print("File not found. Please check the file path.")
except PermissionError:
    print("You don't have permission to read this file.")
```

By gracefully handling exceptions, you can build more robust programs that can handle unexpected scenarios.

Conclusion
```

Reading files in Python is straightforward but versatile. Whether you need to read a simple text file or handle more complex file-reading tasks, Python's built-in functions and modules provide all the tools you need. Practice these techniques to become efficient at handling files in your Python projects.

Writing Files

When it comes to working with files in Python, one essential task you'll often encounter is writing data to a file. This subchapter will guide you through the process of writing files, providing pertinent information and practical examples to help you grasp this fundamental concept.

The Basics of Writing Files

In Python, writing to a file is straightforward. The most commonly used function for this purpose is `open()`. The `open()` function is versatile and can handle both reading from and writing to files. To begin writing, you typically need to open the file in one of the following modes:
- `'w'`: Write mode. If the file already exists, its contents will be truncated (erased) before writing begins. If the file doesn't exist, it will be created.

- `"a"`: Append mode. Writes data to the end of the file without truncating it. If the file doesn't exist, it will be created.

Writing to a File in Write Mode

Here is a basic example of writing to a file in write mode:

```python
# Open a file in write mode
with open('example.txt', 'w') as file:
    # Write data to the file
    file.write('Hello, world!\n')
    file.write('This is a new line in the file.\n')
```

In this example:
1. We open `example.txt` in write mode using `with open('example.txt', 'w') as file:`.
2. The `with` statement ensures that the file is properly closed after the block of code is executed.
3. The `file.write()` method is used to write strings to the file. Each call to `write()` appends the provided text immediately after the last character written unless the file is opened in a different mode or the position index in the file is moved manually.

Writing Multiple Lines

If you need to write multiple lines, you could write them individually using the `write()` method in a loop. However, there's a more convenient method called `writelines()`, which can take a list of strings and write them to the file.

```python
lines = [
    'First line of the file.\n',
    'Second line of the file.\n',
    'Third line of the file.\n'
]

with open('example.txt', 'w') as file:
    file.writelines(lines)
```

Appending to a File

Sometimes, you might want to add content to an existing file without deleting the existing data. To achieve this, you use append mode (`'a'`). Here's how you can do it:

```python
new_lines = [
    'Fourth line of the file.\n',
    'Fifth line of the file.\n'
]

with open('example.txt', 'a') as file:
    file.writelines(new_lines)
```

In this example, `example.txt` will retain its previous content, and the new lines will be added at the end of the file.

Dealing with Different Data Types

Often, the data you want to write to a file isn't just plain text—it could be numbers, objects, or other data types. In such cases, you need to convert these data types to strings before writing them to a file. For instance:

```python
numbers = [10, 20, 30, 40, 50]
```

```python
with open('numbers.txt', 'w') as file:
    for number in numbers:
        file.write(f'{number}\n')
```

In this example, each number is converted to a string and written to a new line in `numbers.txt`.

File Encoding

When dealing with text files, encoding is an important consideration, especially if your file contains non-ASCII characters. The `open()` function allows you to specify an encoding:

```python
text_with_non_ascii = 'Olá, mundo!'

with open('example_utf8.txt', 'w', encoding='utf-8') as file:
    file.write(text_with_non_ascii)
```

By specifying `encoding='utf-8'`, Python ensures that the file is written using UTF-8 encoding, which is a widely used encoding standard for text files.

Error Handling

While working with file operations, handling potential errors is crucial. What if the file cannot be opened or written to? The `try...except` blocks can be used to manage such situations gracefully:

```python
try:
    with open('non_existing_dir/example.txt', 'w') as file:
        file.write('This might cause an IOError.')
except IOError as e:
    print(f"An error occurred: {e}")
```

By using a `try...except` block, we can catch and handle any IOError that might occur, such as attempting to write to a non-existing directory.

With these examples and explanations, you should have a solid foundation for writing files in Python. Whether you're saving user input, logging information, or generating reports, understanding these concepts will prove invaluable in your programming journey.

File Modes

When it comes to working with files in Python, understanding file modes is crucial. File modes determine the actions you can perform on a file, such as reading from it, writing to it, appending data, and more. Here, we'll delve into the most commonly used file modes and their purposes.

1. **Read Mode ('r')**

The read mode is the default mode for opening files in Python. When you open a file in read mode, you can read its contents, but you cannot modify it. Here's a basic example:

```python
with open('example.txt', 'r') as file:
    content = file.read()
    print(content)
```

If the specified file does not exist, Python will raise an `IOError`.

2. **Write Mode ('w')**

Write mode is used for writing to a file. When you open a file in write mode, the file's existing content is erased, and a new file is created if it doesn't already exist. This mode is ideal when you want to start fresh with new content.

```python
with open('example.txt', 'w') as file:
    file.write("Hello, World!")
```

Be cautious with this mode to avoid unintentional data loss.

3. **Append Mode ('a')**

The append mode opens a file for writing, but instead of erasing existing content, it adds new data to the end of the file. Use this mode when you want to preserve the original data while adding new information.

```python
with open('example.txt', 'a') as file:
    file.write("\nAppended line.")
```

4. **Read and Write Mode ('r+')**

This mode allows you to both read from and write to a file. The file must exist, and unlike in write mode, the file's content is not erased upon opening. This mode provides greater flexibility.

```python
with open('example.txt', 'r+') as file:
    content = file.read()
    file.write("\nNew line added.")
```

```

5. **Write and Read Mode ('w+')**

Write and read mode allows you to read and write a file, but like 'w', it truncates the file content first. If the file does not exist, it creates a new one.

```python
with open('example.txt', 'w+') as file:
    file.write("Starting fresh.")
    file.seek(0)
    content = file.read()
    print(content)
```

6. **Append and Read Mode ('a+')**

This mode opens a file for both appending and reading. If the file does not exist, a new file is created. Existing data is preserved, and new data is added to the end.

```python
with open('example.txt', 'a+') as file:
    file.write("Appending yet another line.\n")
    file.seek(0)
    content = file.read()
    print(content)
```
```

```

7. **Binary Modes ('rb', 'wb', 'ab', 'r+b', 'w+b', 'a+b')**

All the modes mentioned above can be quickly adapted for binary files by appending a 'b' to the mode string. Binary modes are necessary when dealing with non-text files such as images or executable files.

```python
with open('image.png', 'rb') as binary_file:
    data = binary_file.read()

with open('image.png', 'wb') as binary_file:
    binary_file.write(data)
```

Learning to choose the appropriate file mode is integral to effective file handling in Python. Each mode caters to different scenarios, allowing you to read, write, and manage files with precision and control. Understanding these modes will elevate your Python programming and enable you to work with a variety of file types and operations seamlessly.

Handling File Exceptions

Handling File Exceptions
```

When working with files in Python, it's almost inevitable that you'll encounter some kind of error or exception at some point. These can range from trying to open a file that doesn't exist to attempting to write to a file you don't have permission to change. Handling file exceptions gracefully is crucial for building robust programs that don't crash unexpectedly.

Common File-Related Exceptions

1. **FileNotFoundError**: This exception is thrown when trying to open a file that does not exist. It's useful to catch this exception to prompt the user or to create a new file.
2. **PermissionError**: This occurs when you try to read or write to a file without the appropriate permissions. For example, trying to write to a read-only file will trigger this exception.
3. **IsADirectoryError**: If you attempt to perform a file-related task on a directory, like opening it as a file, Python will raise this exception.
4. **IOError**: This is a more general exception that covers any kind of Input/Output error which doesn't fall into the above categories.

The Try-Except Block

Python's `try-except` block allows you to handle exceptions in a clean and efficient way. Let's look at an example of how to handle a `FileNotFoundError`:

```python
try:
    with open('non_existent_file.txt', 'r') as file:
        content = file.read()
except FileNotFoundError:
    print("The file you are trying to read does not exist. Please check the file name and try again.")
```

In this example, if the file `non_existent_file.txt` does not exist, the `FileNotFoundError` exception is caught and an appropriate message is printed.

Multiple Exceptions

Sometimes, you may want to handle multiple exceptions in the same block. Python allows you to catch multiple exceptions by specifying them as a tuple within the `except` statement.

```python
```

```python
try:
    with open('important_file.txt', 'r') as file:
        content = file.read()
except (FileNotFoundError, PermissionError) as e:
    print(f"An error occurred: {e}")
```

In this case, both `FileNotFoundError` and `PermissionError` are caught, and the specific error message is printed.

The Else Clause

You can add an `else` clause after your `try-except` block to execute code when no exceptions are raised. This is useful for separating the error-catching logic from the main logic of your code.

```python
try:
    with open('existing_file.txt', 'r') as file:
        content = file.read()
except FileNotFoundError:
    print("The file does not exist.")
else:
    print("File read successfully.")
```

```

In this scenario, the success message "File read successfully." will only be printed if no exceptions are raised.

#### The Finally Clause

The `finally` block can be used to specify cleanup actions that must be performed under all circumstances, such as closing a file.

```python
try:
    file = open('some_file.txt', 'r')
    content = file.read()
except FileNotFoundError:
    print("The file does not exist.")
finally:
    file.close()
```

Whether an exception occurs or not, the `finally` block ensures that the file is closed properly, preventing resource leaks.

Raising Your Own Exceptions
```

In some cases, you might want to raise a custom exception when a specific condition is met. This can be done using the `raise` statement:

```python
def read_file(filename):
    if not filename.endswith('.txt'):
        raise ValueError("Only '.txt' files are supported.")
    with open(filename, 'r') as file:
        return file.read()

try:
    content = read_file('document.pdf')
except ValueError as e:
    print(f"An error occurred: {e}")
```

Here, if a non-text file is passed to `read_file`, a `ValueError` is raised and subsequently caught in the `try-except` block.

By understanding and effectively handling file exceptions, you can ensure that your programs are more reliable and maintainable. Good exception handling not only helps in identifying the root cause of errors but also improves user experience by providing meaningful messages and actions when something goes wrong.

Working with CSV Files

When it comes to working with files in Python, one of the most common file formats you'll encounter is the CSV file. CSV stands for Comma-Separated Values, and these files are a simple and convenient way to store tabular data. Each line in a CSV file corresponds to a row in the table, and columns within that row are separated by commas.

CSV files are popular because they provide a text-based way to represent complex data. They're easily created and read by both humans and machines, making them a versatile choice for data storage and transfer.

Reading CSV Files

Python's built-in `csv` module provides functions to both read from and write to CSV files. Let's start with reading CSV files. Suppose you have a CSV file named `example.csv` with the following content:

```

Name,Age,Occupation
```

```
Alice,30,Engineer
Bob,25,Data Scientist
Charlie,35,Teacher
```

To read this file in Python, you can use the following code:

```python
import csv

with open('example.csv', mode='r') as file:
    csv_reader = csv.reader(file)
    for row in csv_reader:
        print(row)
```

The `csv.reader` function reads each row of the CSV file and returns it as a list. When you run this script, the output will be:

```
['Name', 'Age', 'Occupation']
['Alice', '30', 'Engineer']
['Bob', '25', 'Data Scientist']
['Charlie', '35', 'Teacher']
```

```

### Using a CSV DictReader

If you prefer to work with dictionaries, where the first row of the CSV file is treated as the header, you can use `DictReader`. Here's how you can read the file in that manner:

```python
import csv

with open('example.csv', mode='r') as file:
    csv_reader = csv.DictReader(file)
    for row in csv_reader:
        print(row)
```

In this case, each `row` is an ordered dictionary that maps column names to the corresponding data values. The output will be:

```

{'Name': 'Alice', 'Age': '30', 'Occupation': 'Engineer'}
{'Name': 'Bob', 'Age': '25', 'Occupation': 'Data Scientist'}
{'Name': 'Charlie', 'Age': '35', 'Occupation': 'Teacher'}

```

Writing to CSV Files

Writing to a CSV file is equally straightforward. You can use `csv.writer` to write rows to a CSV file. For example:

```python
import csv

data = [
    ['Name', 'Age', 'Occupation'],
    ['Alice', '30', 'Engineer'],
    ['Bob', '25', 'Data Scientist'],
    ['Charlie', '35', 'Teacher']
]

with open('output.csv', mode='w', newline='') as file:
    csv_writer = csv.writer(file)
    csv_writer.writerows(data)
```

This code writes the `data` list to `output.csv`. The `newline=''` parameter is essential to prevent the `csv` module from adding an
```

extra newline between rows on Windows.

Using a CSV DictWriter

If you want to write data as dictionaries, use `DictWriter`. Here's an example that demonstrates how to do this:

```python
import csv

data = [
    {'Name': 'Alice', 'Age': 30, 'Occupation': 'Engineer'},
    {'Name': 'Bob', 'Age': 25, 'Occupation': 'Data Scientist'},
    {'Name': 'Charlie', 'Age': 35, 'Occupation': 'Teacher'}
]

with open('output_dict.csv', mode='w', newline='') as file:
    fieldnames = ['Name', 'Age', 'Occupation']
    csv_writer = csv.DictWriter(file, fieldnames=fieldnames)

    csv_writer.writeheader()
    csv_writer.writerows(data)
```

This script writes the data as a CSV file named `output_dict.csv` with the same header and rows as shown in the previous reading example.

Conclusion

Working with CSV files in Python is effortless with the `csv` module. Whether you're reading from or writing to CSV files, understanding both `csv.reader` and `csv.DictReader` for reading, and `csv.writer` and `csv.DictWriter` for writing, will make your data processing experience smooth. As you continue to work with Python, you'll find that these tools make CSV files a robust and flexible format for data interchange.

JSON Files

In the world of Python programming, working with different file formats is a crucial skill. Among the various file types you'll encounter, JSON (JavaScript Object Notation) files are especially common due to their simplicity and readability. JSON is widely used for data interchange between applications, making it an indispensable tool for any programmer's toolkit.

JSON is essentially a lightweight format that is easy for humans to read and write, and easy for machines to parse and generate. Here, we'll delve into how you can effectively read from and write to JSON files using Python.

Reading from a JSON File

To read JSON data from a file, you typically use Python's built-in `json` module. Here's a step-by-step example to get you started:

1. **Import the json module**:

    ```python
    import json
    ```

2. **Open the JSON file**: Use the `open` function to open the file. In this case, let's assume you have a file called `data.json`.

    ```python
    with open('data.json', 'r') as file:
        data = json.load(file)
    ```

3. **Accessing the JSON data**: Once loaded, `data` becomes a Python dictionary or list, depending on the structure of the JSON file.

You can now interact with this data just like any other Python data structures.

```python
print(data)  # This could print a dictionary or list
```

Writing to a JSON File

Writing JSON data to a file is just as straightforward. The `json` module provides the `dump` method for this purpose. Here's an example:

1. **Prepare your data**: Ensure your data is in a format that JSON can handle, such as dictionaries or lists.

```python
data_to_write = {
    "name": "John Doe",
    "age": 30,
    "city": "New York"
}
```

2. **Open the file for writing**:

```python
with open('output.json', 'w') as file:
    json.dump(data_to_write, file, indent=4)
```

The `indent=4` argument is optional but useful as it formats the JSON with four spaces of indentation, making it more readable.

Common Pitfalls

While working with JSON files, you might encounter a few common issues:

- **Incorrect JSON Formatting**: If your JSON file is not properly formatted, `json.load` will raise a `ValueError`. Always ensure the JSON you're trying to read is valid.
- **Encoding Issues**: When dealing with different languages or special characters, be mindful of encoding. The `open` function allows you to specify encoding, like so:

```python
with open('data.json', 'r', encoding='utf-8') as file:
```

```
    data = json.load(file)
```

- **File Not Found**: If the file you're trying to read doesn't exist, Python will raise a `FileNotFoundError`. Using a `try...except` block can help you handle such cases gracefully.

Advanced Usage

For more complex tasks, Python's `json` module offers additional functionality:

- **Serialization**: Custom objects can be serialized to JSON by defining how they should be converted to a JSON-serializable format. This is done by creating a custom method in your class and passing it to `json.dump`.

```python
class Employee:
    def __init__(self, name, age):
        self.name = name
        self.age = age

    def to_json(self):
```

```
        return {"name": self.name, "age": self.age}

emp = Employee("Alice", 28)
with open('employee.json', 'w') as file:
    json.dump(emp.to_json(), file)
```

- **Deserialization**: Similarly, you can customize how JSON data is converted back into Python objects.

```python
def from_json(data):
    return Employee(data["name"], data["age"])

with open('employee.json', 'r') as file:
    data = json.load(file)
    emp = from_json(data)
```

By mastering these fundamental operations, you'll be well-equipped to handle JSON files in Python with ease, making your data handling tasks more efficient and effective.

Best Practices

When working with files in Python, adhering to best practices is crucial for ensuring your code is efficient, maintainable, and error-free. Here, we'll discuss some of these best practices to guide you on your coding journey.

1. Use Context Managers:

One of the fundamental practices is to use context managers when opening files. Using the `with` statement ensures that files are properly closed after their suite is executed, even if an exception is raised. This helps in resource management and avoids potential memory leaks. For example:

```python
with open('example.txt', 'r') as file:
    content = file.read()
# No need to call file.close()
```

2. Specify Modes Explicitly:

Always specify the mode in which you are opening the file (`'r'` for reading, `'w'` for writing, `'a'` for appending, etc.). This makes your code clearer and avoids accidental writes or overwrites.

```python
```

```python
# Reading Mode
with open('example.txt', 'r') as file:
    content = file.read()

# Writing Mode
with open('example.txt', 'w') as file:
    file.write("Hello, World!")
```

3. Handle Exceptions:

Files operations can fail for various reasons, such as file not found or permission issues. Handle possible exceptions using `try` and `except` blocks to make your program robust.

```python
try:
    with open('example.txt', 'r') as file:
        content = file.read()
except FileNotFoundError:
    print("The file does not exist.")
except IOError:
    print("An IOError has occurred.")
```

4. Use Binary Mode for Non-Text Files:

When dealing with non-text files, such as images or executables, open files in binary mode by appending `b` to the mode. This prevents encoding-related issues.

```python
with open('image.png', 'rb') as file:
    content = file.read()
```

5. Read and Write Efficiently:

When handling large files, reading or writing in chunks can be more efficient than reading or writing the entire file at once.

```python
# Reading in chunks
with open('largefile.txt', 'r') as file:
    while True:
        chunk = file.read(1024)  # Read in chunks of 1024 bytes
        if not chunk:
            break
        process(chunk)

# Writing in chunks
```

```python
data = ['line1\n', 'line2\n', 'line3\n']
with open('output.txt', 'w') as file:
    for line in data:
        file.write(line)
```

6. Use `os` and `pathlib` Modules:

For file path manipulations and more advanced file operations, leverage the `os` and `pathlib` modules. They provide powerful, platform-independent ways to handle files and directories.

```python
from pathlib import Path

# Using pathlib
path = Path('example.txt')
if path.exists():
    print(f"{path} exists.")

import os

# Using os module
if os.path.exists('example.txt'):
    print("example.txt exists.")
```

```

**7. Consider Encoding:**

Always specify the encoding when working with text files to avoid encoding issues, especially when dealing with non-ASCII text.

```python
with open('example.txt', 'r', encoding='utf-8') as file:
    content = file.read()
```

By following these best practices, you can ensure that your file-handling operations in Python are both efficient and safe, minimizing the risk of errors and making your codebase more maintainable.
```

Conclusion

Review of Key Concepts

As we draw this journey through Python programming to a close, it's essential to reflect on the key concepts we've explored. Revisiting these foundational elements will reinforce your understanding and ensure you're well-prepared for further adventures in coding.

First and foremost, we began with variables and data types. These building blocks are the heart of any programming language. Variables act as containers for storing data values, while data types (such as integers, floats, strings, and booleans) define what kind of data we're working with. Understanding how Python handles different data types allows you to manipulate variables and craft more complex programs.

Next, we delved into control structures, the backbone of Python logic. Conditional statements (if, elif, and else) enable programs to make decisions based on given conditions. Looping constructs (for and while loops) allow you to iterate over data, repeating operations as needed until a condition is met. Mastering these control structures helps you create dynamic and responsive code.

Following that, functions were introduced as a way to bundle chunks of code into reusable blocks. Defined with the def keyword, functions make our code more organized and modular. By passing arguments to functions and returning values, we can create versatile scripts that are easier to debug, maintain, and extend.

Once comfortable with functions, we then tackled the concept of objects and classes, the cornerstones of Object-Oriented Programming (OOP). By defining classes, you create blueprints for objects, encapsulating data and behaviors together. This paradigm not only fosters code reusability but also aligns your scripts with real-world modeling, making programming more intuitive.

And of course, no Python journey would be complete without touching on modules and packages. We explored how to use built-in modules as well as how to create custom ones. This understanding expands the functionality of your programs exponentially, allowing you to leverage a rich ecosystem of existing Python libraries.

Throughout our exploration, we consistently emphasized best practices, such as writing clean and readable code, using comments effectively, and employing version control systems like Git. These habits are indispensable for professional development and ensure that your projects remain manageable as they grow in complexity.

In summary, our Python 101 journey has equipped you with a firm grasp of essential programming constructs. By mastering variables, control structures, functions, OOP, and modules, you've laid a robust foundation on which to build more sophisticated Python projects. As you move forward, keep experimenting, stay curious, and don't hesitate to revisit these foundational concepts whenever needed. Happy coding!

Advanced Topics to Explore

As we draw this journey through Python to a close, it's important to recognize that our exploration doesn't end here. We've covered the essentials and gained a solid foundation, but there's a wide world of advanced topics waiting to be discovered. Delving deeper can elevate your skills, opening doors to more complex projects and professional opportunities. Here, we'll briefly touch on a few advanced topics that you may find particularly intriguing and beneficial.

The first area to explore is **Decorators and Metaclasses**. These powerful features enable metaprogramming, allowing you to modify the behavior of classes or functions at runtime. Mastering decorators can streamline your code, enhance reusability, and implement aspect-oriented programming aspects with ease. Meanwhile, metaclasses provide deeper control over class creation, crucial for creating frameworks or libraries.

Next up is **Concurrency and Parallelism**. As applications become more resource-intensive, understanding how to write efficient, concurrent code is invaluable. Python offers several libraries and constructs, like threading, multiprocessing, and asyncio, to help you manage concurrent execution. Grasping these could help you optimize performance significantly, especially in data processing or real-time systems.

Network Programming is another rewarding domain. Python's `socket` library facilitates low-level networking, whereas frameworks like `Twisted` and `asyncio` offer high-level abstractions for writing servers and clients. In an age where interconnected systems prevail, skills in network programming enable you to develop robust services and improve inter-application communication.

Moreover, if you're interested in the under-the-hood workings of Python, learning about **Python's C API** can be enlightening. This knowledge allows you to write Python extensions in C or C++, enhance performance-critical sections of your applications, and gain insights into Python's internals regarding memory management and execution model.

Also worth exploring is **Machine Learning and Data Science**.

Libraries like TensorFlow, PyTorch, and Scikit-learn make Python a powerhouse in these fields. From crafting intelligent algorithms to analyzing vast datasets, the applications are endless. This sector is booming and offers tremendous potential for those adept in Python.

Lastly, delve into **Cryptography and Security**. In the sphere of secure communications, Python's libraries like `cryptography` and `PyCrypto` are invaluable. Understanding the principles of encryption, digital signatures, and secure hashing can empower you to build secure applications, safeguarding data integrity and privacy.

These advanced topics not only strengthen your understanding of Python but also enable you to solve diverse, complex problems with elegance. As you continue your learning journey, challenge yourself with these areas, participate in open-source projects, and keep pushing the boundaries of what you can achieve with Python. The horizon of knowledge is vast, and every step you take in these advanced topics will illuminate new, exciting vistas in your programming career.

Python Community and Resources

As we draw this journey through Python to a close, it is essential to recognize the vibrant and ever-growing Python community and the wealth of resources available to you. The Python community is one of the most supportive and diverse ecosystems in the programming world. Whether you're a novice stepping into the world of coding or an experienced developer looking to hone your skills further, there are ample avenues to explore and immerse yourself within this community.

Firstly, the role of open-source is pivotal in the Python community. Python itself is an open-source language, which means it thrives on collaboration, shared knowledge, and collective improvement. Platforms like GitHub and GitLab host thousands of Python projects where you can contribute, learn from others' code, and even find inspiration for your own projects. Don't hesitate to jump into these repositories, submit pull requests, or even fork your own versions to experiment and create.

Additionally, forums and discussion boards serve as excellent resources. Websites such as Stack Overflow, Reddit's r/learnpython, and the Python community on Quora are bustling with activity. Here, you can ask questions, share insights, and participate in discussions that range from basic syntax issues to advanced machine learning techniques. Don't be afraid to ask for help; the Python community is known for being remarkably welcoming and patient with beginners.

For those who prefer a more structured learning path, numerous courses are available online. Platforms like Coursera, edX, and Udacity offer courses that can cater to your learning style and schedule. Furthermore, sites like Python.org, Real Python, and Full Stack Python provide in-depth tutorials, guides, and latest news relevant to the Python ecosystem. These resources can help reinforce your learning and keep you updated on new developments within the language.

Meetups and conferences also play a significant role in the Python landscape. PyCon, the international Python conference, is an excellent opportunity to network with fellow Python enthusiasts, attend workshops, and see how Python is being applied in various industries. Local Python user groups and regional conferences also offer more opportunities to connect with peers in your area and learn from industry experts.

Books and online documentation are indispensable resources as well. "Automate the Boring Stuff with Python" by Al Sweigart and "Python Crash Course" by Eric Matthes are highly recommended for beginners. The official Python documentation is also an essential resource that you'll find yourself returning to frequently. It provides comprehensive and authoritative information on the language's features and standard library.

Moreover, don't underestimate the power of social media and podcasts. Twitter, LinkedIn, and YouTube have countless influencers, educators, and communities dedicated to Python. Podcasts like "Talk Python To Me" and "Python Bytes" can be perfect for keeping up with the latest trends and insights in Python, especially when time is a constraint.

Finally, contributing to the community is just as crucial as benefiting from it. Write blog posts, share your projects, participate in hackathons, or even start teaching others. Sharing your knowledge and experiences not only helps others but also solidifies your understanding and opens doors to new opportunities.

In essence, the Python community is a rich tapestry of knowledge, collaboration, and growth. As you continue your journey with Python, remember that you are never alone. The resources mentioned are merely a starting point; the actual potential lies in how actively and passionately you engage with the community. Embrace the philosophy of learning together and contributing back, and you will undoubtedly find your place and flourish within the Python ecosystem.

Building Real-World Projects

As we near the end of our journey through Python 101, it's crucial to emphasize one of the most valuable lessons any coder can learn: putting theory into practice by building real-world projects. This transition from learning concepts to applying them is where true proficiency and mastery begin to take shape.

Why is building real-world projects so important? First and foremost, it allows you to consolidate your knowledge and see how different parts of the Python language and libraries come together to solve problems. It's one thing to learn about loops, functions, and modules in isolation, but it's another thing entirely to integrate these tools to create something functional.

Moreover, tackling projects exposes you to a variety of challenges and edge cases that textbook examples often overlook. When you embark on a project, you are likely to encounter bugs, unexpected behaviors, and performance issues. Learning to debug, optimize, and refactor your code in response to these challenges is an invaluable skill that will serve you well in any programming endeavor.

Another advantage of building real-world projects is the opportunity to work with external libraries and APIs. While we have covered many built-in Python modules in this book, the Python ecosystem is rich with third-party libraries that extend its capabilities. Whether you are building a web application with Django, analyzing data with Pandas, or creating visualizations with Matplotlib, leveraging these libraries can significantly speed up development and open new possibilities for your projects.

Additionally, real-world projects offer a platform for collaboration. Whether you are contributing to an open-source project, working on a team at your job, or simply sharing your code on GitHub, collaboration teaches you to write clean, maintainable code. It also helps you become comfortable with version control systems like Git, code reviews, and documentation—skills that are essential for any professional developer.

Finally, completing projects gives you a tangible outcome that you can showcase to potential employers, clients, or fellow developers. Your portfolio of projects demonstrates your ability to apply your skills in practical settings and your commitment to continual learning and improvement.

So, where should you start? Begin by identifying a problem you are passionate about or a tool you wish existed. It doesn't have to be groundbreaking or original; even small projects can provide significant learning experiences. From there, outline the features and requirements, and start building incrementally. Don't be afraid to ask for help, seek feedback, and iterate on your design.

To aid you in this journey, consider joining online communities, attending local meetups, or participating in hackathons. These environments provide support, inspiration, and sometimes even mentorship.

In conclusion, while this book has aimed to equip you with the foundational knowledge of Python, it's your projects that will truly refine your skills and deepen your understanding. Embrace the challenges, be persistent, and enjoy the satisfaction that comes from solving real problems with code. Happy coding!

Maintaining and Improving Your Skills

As you reach the end of this journey through Python 101, it's essential to reflect on the path ahead. Mastering Python, or any programming language, is an ongoing process. Like any skill, it requires regular practice, a willingness to tackle new challenges, and a mindset geared towards continual learning. Here are some strategies to help you maintain and sharpen your Python skills long after you've read this book.

First and foremost, make coding a habit. Your proficiency with Python will grow if you code regularly, even if it's just for a few minutes each day. Regular practice will help cement the concepts you've learned and make it easier to take on more complex projects over time. Consider maintaining a coding journal where you track your progress, list topics you need to revisit, and note down interesting new things you encounter.

Next, immerse yourself in the vibrant Python community. Whether through forums like Stack Overflow, subreddits such as r/learnpython, or local meetups and hackathons, being part of a community offers countless benefits. Not only can you seek help when you're stuck, but you can also gain insights into different coding styles and paradigms. You'll also have the chance to help others, which is a fantastic way to reinforce your own knowledge.

Another excellent way to maintain and improve your Python skills is by contributing to open-source projects. Open-source contributions offer real-world coding experience, the chance to collaborate with more experienced programmers, and the satisfaction of knowing your work benefits others. Websites like GitHub provide a platform to find projects that align with your interests and skill level. Start by tackling issues tagged for beginners and as you gain confidence, move on to more challenging tasks.

Don't underestimate the power of teaching. Whether it's writing blog posts, creating YouTube tutorials, or merely explaining concepts to a friend or colleague, teaching others is a powerful way to reinforce your learning. Articulating your thoughts helps solidify your own understanding and might even provide new insights or perspectives on the material.

Then, keep your knowledge fresh and up-to-date by following Python's evolution. The language and its libraries are continually evolving, with updates that add features and optimize performance. Make it a habit to read the release notes of new Python versions and familiarize yourself with the changes. Also, stay informed about new libraries and tools that can simplify tasks or extend Python's capabilities.

Consider taking on personal projects that excite you. Whether it's building a game, developing a web application, or automating a personal task, personal projects are a great way to apply what you've learned while pursuing something you're passionate about. These projects not only solidify your understanding but also provide a tangible portfolio of your skills, which can be showcased to potential employers or collaborators.

Remember, no journey in coding is without its challenges. When you encounter obstacles, treat them as opportunities to learn. Don't be disheartened by bugs or errors; instead, see them as puzzles waiting to be solved. The skills you develop in debugging and problem-solving are invaluable and will serve you well in any programming endeavor.

Finally, never lose the curiosity and enthusiasm that brought you to Python in the first place. The world of programming is vast, with endless possibilities for what you can create and achieve. Keep exploring, stay curious, and always push the boundaries of what you think you can do. With diligence and passion, your Python skills will not only be maintained but will flourish and lead you to new heights in your coding journey.

Index

Introduction: Page 2

What is Python?: Page 2

History and Evolution: Page 4

Why Learn Python?: Page 7

Setting Up the Python Environment: Page 9

Your First Python Program: Page 14

Chapter 1: Basics of Python: Page 18

Variables and Data Types: Page 18

Basic Operators: Page 23

Conditional Statements: Page 30

Loops: Page 35

Comments: Page 40

Indentation and Code Blocks: Page 43

Basic Input and Output: Page 46

Chapter 2: Data Structures: Page 51

Lists: Page 51

Tuples: Page 55

Dictionaries: Page 60

Sets: Page 66

String Manipulation: Page 72

List Comprehensions: Page 77

Dictionary Comprehensions: Page 82

Chapter 3: Functions and Modules: Page 88

Defining and Calling Functions: Page 88
Function Arguments: Page 94
Return Statement: Page 99
Lambda Functions: Page 103
Importing Modules: Page 108
Standard Library Modules: Page 113
Creating Your Own Modules: Page 120
Chapter 4: Object-Oriented Programming: Page 126
Classes and Objects: Page 126
Attributes and Methods: Page 131
Inheritance: Page 137
Polymorphism: Page 143
Encapsulation: Page 148
Magic Methods: Page 151
Using OOP in Real Projects: Page 156
Chapter 5: Exception Handling and Debugging: Page 162
Understanding Exceptions: Page 162
Try and Except Blocks: Page 167
Finally and Else Clauses: Page 173
Raising Exceptions: Page 178
Custom Exceptions: Page 183
Debugging Techniques: Page 188

Using pdb for Debugging: Page 195
Chapter 6: Working with Files: Page 201
Reading Files: Page 201
Writing Files: Page 206
File Modes: Page 211
Handling File Exceptions: Page 215
Working with CSV Files: Page 221
JSON Files: Page 226
Best Practices: Page 231
Conclusion: Page 237
Review of Key Concepts: Page 237
Advanced Topics to Explore: Page 239
Python Community and Resources: Page 241
Building Real-World Projects: Page 244
Maintaining and Improving Your Skills: Page 247

Printed in Great Britain
by Amazon